MOUNT

SUMMIT GRIN

This Grin Can Be Yours!

HIKING TALL

Mount Whitney In A Day
Third Edition

Marvin D Cope

Planning, Preparing, and Making a Great, Memorable Hike on Mount Whitney

ABOUT THE COVER

The cover is composed of a sunrise photograph just below Trail Camp on the Mount Whitney Trail. The image of Mount Whitney is embedded in a headlamp photo on the Mount Whitney Trail.

DEDICATION

Several people helped me to experience the Mount Whitney hike and subsequently help me share my learning with you to help prepare you for this great hike. This book is dedicated:

To my wife, Brynn, who has unconditionally supported me to hike Mt. Whitney.

To Chris and Susie Gonaver, who allowed me to tag along with their group from San Diego on my first Mt. Whitney hike.

The Gonaver Group

To my friend, Roger Thorsvold, who shared with me his own hiking experience on Mt. Whitney and planting the idea on my "bucket list."

To my friend, Robert Farrell, who surprised me with a banner and dinner on completion of my first Mt. Whitney hike.

Congratulations Banner on Car

To my friend, Pradeep Sharma, for having the trust to hike with me on my third Mt. Whitney hike.

Pradeep Sharma and Marv Group

To my friends, Ron Upson and Sam Moore, who made the hike with me in 2012 to honor their friend, Christian Meining, who passed while hiking Mt. Whitney in November, 2010. Ron and Sam were kind enough to allow me to use many of their pictures.

Ron Upson Group

To my friend, Betzy Farrell, and to my wife, Brynn Cope for proofing reading the book.

In memory of LE Spalding, my previous boss, who inspired me to be the best I can be instead of just reaching a goal.

To my friend, John Linn for editing this book.

WHY HIKE MT. WHITNEY?

In my work career, I have always looked for a means to lead in some way that would set me apart from the group. I actually found that hiking Mt. Whitney did that for me in my personal life.

If you are competitive, if you like accomplishments, if you like to earn attention, if you like doing something many others either can't or will not even try to accomplish then hiking Mt. Whitney may be the perfect hike for you.

Older adults all the way down to children hike this mountain. It can be done in two to three days at a much more leisurely pace than I will discuss in this book.

For competitive people, this hike will be every bit as challenging as a long race. The physical demand and needed stamina will hold its own when discussing races or marathons.

There is only one mountain in the United States that is higher than Mt. Whitney and that is Denali or Mt. McKinley in Alaska. That hike requires specific mountaineering skills and is certainly not going to be done in one day. This is the highest mountain in the contiguous U.S. and with basic physical training and planning it can be hiked in one day.

When you talk to your friends regarding the 22-mile trek up and down a 14,505 foot mountain in one day, you will have your friend's attention. Some people will have a difficult time understanding the need to walk 22 miles on level ground, but adding in the 6,140 foot elevation climb and then descent, takes this accomplishment over the top.

Only you know what drives you and what you are looking to accomplish in life and I have found this hike is quite gratifying.

TABLE OF CONTENTS

FORWARD:

My goal in this book is to help you "feel" the experience of hiking Mt. Whitney in a day and decide if this trip is for you. My aim is to prepare you for your hike so that it is a pleasant experience with the main surprises coming from nature and not from you being unprepared.

You may feel this book presents a rather negative or dark side of hiking Mt. Whitney. I would rather talk those out of making this hike than find them in trouble because they were unprepared and unaware of the dangers. I don't want to make you afraid of making the hike but to respect the perils of the mountain.

I reference this event as a "hike" and not a climb since I feel it is a feat available to all those willing to prepare and attempt it. I will only guide you on preparation of the Mt. Whitney Trail, the easiest hike on the mountain. There are other trails that can take you right up the face of the mount, requiring true rock-climbing experience. This is not one of those.

Just to be clear, there are several companies that will take you on multiday trips to camp out on the mountain and hike it. They will, of course do this for a fee. You may decide to get some friends to plan a multiday trip. There are other books that are better suited to help you prepare for a multiday hike. I will totally focus on helping you plan, prepare and hike Mt. Whitney in one day. That does NOT mean the whole adventure will be in one day, only the main hike. I am a rather impatient person and do not relish the idea of hiking a few thousand feet and then setting up camp for a day, waiting for the next day to hike again. I like to get there, hike it and go back home.

I have hiked Mt. Whitney four times at this writing and am planning my fifth in July, 2013. My first trip was with a fairly large group; my second was solo; my third hike was with a friend and my last hike was with a group of five. I have made some mistakes that I will share. I will also share what I have learned from past mistakes so you can hopefully avoid making the same ones. Many people attempt to hike Mt. Whitney and fail. In all fairness, the failures may be from hikers experiencing altitude sickness, hypothermia, being in inadequate physical condition, poor timing by starting too late, weather, dehydration, accidents, insufficient planning or inadequate food to support the rigorous demands of the hike. My purpose is to give you the necessary information to get a "Mount Whitney Summit Grin."

The first objective of this book is to help you get a permit for the hike as soon as possible. It will then give you some of my first-hand hiking experiences so you can get the "feel" of the hike. Thirdly, it will help you understand concerns you should have and how to properly prepare for the hike. Fourthly, it will give you an equipment list and ideas of what to look for when purchasing items. Lastly, it will give you some background information of the mountain range's origin and history.

In sharing my ideas, readings and research, I do not take on the responsibility for your safety to hike Mt. Whitney. If you have concerns about hiking this mountain, I suggest you follow those concerns to reach resolution of either feeling better on how to handle the situation or decide the hike is not for you. This hike is in the wilderness and even though you will probably have many, many people hiking the same day as you and or your group, you will need to be prepared, use common sense and take personal responsibility for your own safety.

PREFACE TO THIRD EDITION

The first and second edition of this book was written in 2012. The main focus was to provide the reader a detailed guide on obtaining a permit to hike Mount Whitney, plan the hike, and be sufficiently informed about the hike to have a great time with few surprises.

I hiked Mount Whitney after my second edition and wanted to add more pictures to better explain the hike. Secondly, I wanted to expand on more information such as Giardia lamblia, group hiking dynamics and back-tracking rules to avoid getting lost or putting oneself in a tough situation.

I wish you excellent weather, clear skies and a fantastic hiking experience. I am interested in any comments or suggestion you may have. Please send to marv.cope@att.net.

LOTTERY FOR PERMITS

My first task is to ask you to check the month and day. . .

IMPORTANT: WHILE YOU ARE READING THIS, YOU MAY BE MISSING AN OPPORTUNITY TO HIKE MT. WHITNEY THIS YEAR!

I make this point to make sure that you don't leisurely read this book and find out that you couldn't get a permit. Read the section regarding permits to determine your urgency. If you are planning on going with others as a group, it may take additional time to determine who can go and when the best times are for your group.

PERMITS

Mt. Whitney is one of the most frequently hiked peaks in the United States. Because of the popularity and need to maintain some order of nature, there are limits to the number of people who are allowed to hike the trails or spend the night on the mountain.[i] Only a maximum of 100 day-hikers are allowed per day. This compares to only 60 multiday hikers, who can camp out on the mountain.[ii] Of the over 30,000 annual hikers and climbers who secure a permit to hike this mountain, approximately **one out of three** hikers will actually reach the summit.[iii]

TIMING FOR PERMITS

November through January

If this month is November, December, January or even February, you have time to plan your group and hike date for an application. The lottery-application process runs from February 1 through March 15. All entries during that time are processed through a lottery to determine the winners of permits for the main hiking season, May through October. These applications may be made online, mail or by phone. Listed below is the contact information:

Inyo National Forest
351 Pacu Lane
Suite 200
Bishop, CA 93514
760-873-2400[iv]

Be advised that there is no particular advantage to sending in your lottery application on February 1 versus March 10. All applications will go into the drawing which is held on March 16 and then processed. After the lottery, a calendar is available at the website, http://www.recreation.gov to see the taken dates and those dates still available. [v]

TYPICAL WEATHER CONDITIONS

The Forest Service describes the Mt. Whitney Trail as *"a non-technical, but strenuous, route to the summit of Mt. Whitney when it is free of snow. Winter mountaineering skills and equipment are necessary for safe travel when snow is on the mountain.*

May – June:

The winter snowpack slowly recedes. Expect snow on the ground above Lone Pine Lake through Memorial Day weekend, and snow on the switchbacks above Trail Camp through June. Nights are usually below freezing. Winter-like storms are still possible. In 2011, there was snow on the trail until July 4.

July –early September:

The trail is usually snow free and weather can be fair and pleasant at elevations above Trail Camp. However, it is often cold and windy. Thunderstorms and lightning are a significant hazard. If thunderstorms are forecasted, plan to leave the summit by noon. Be aware thunderstorms sometimes will occur early in the day. At the first sign of lightning, leave the summit area or exposed ridge tops.

Late September – October:

Short days and cold temperatures make day hikes to the summit difficult. Storms may bring severe cold with high winds and snow deposits from a few inches to several feet. Thin snow may melt quickly, but deeper drifts may linger for the winter. Winter [weather] moun-

taineering equipment and skills are necessary for safe travel when snow is on the mountain.

November – April:

Winter prevails, with deep snow and very cold temperatures. Winter storms may drop several feet of snow and have winds over 100 mph. The road to Whitney Portal is usually closed 8 miles from Lone Pine (at elevation 6,400 ft., about 3 miles from the trailhead) from mid-November to late April. Experienced winter mountaineers should be suitably equipped for extreme conditions and check avalanche conditions and weather forecasts."[vi]

As the Forest Service indicated, the winter months through June may have some deep areas of snow, lasting until mid to late July on the northern faces and shadowed areas on the trail. If you don't want to learn how to maneuver on snow or ice, this may not be the best time for you to hike.

July through September offers much less snow, if any, to just a couple of feet on the shaded and northern faces. Hikers typically have worn a workable trail through the snow for you to follow. The snow patches have typically been about 100 yards in length and from five inches to a couple of feet deep. In mid-July 2011, I had four snow patches on my hike. Two were below Trail Camp, one on the switchbacks and the last just before the summit.

Just as I had three consecutive years with snow on the trail in July, on my fourth hike in 2012, there was very little snow to be found anywhere on the mountain. This particular summer followed a low, rainfall year where the area received about 50% of its normal rainfall. If California is having a wet winter, you may count on snow into July and if it's a dry winter, you may luck out with no snow.

WEEKENDS VERSUS WEEKDAYS

My experience is that weekends are the most popular time for applications. The Forest Service will allow you to apply with 10 alternate dates for your hike. If you really want a weekend for your hike, you may wish to enter those hike dates as early priorities and fill in the rest with weekday hike dates. I found that Wednesdays are probably the easiest to get and of course, Friday through Sunday, the hardest. Remember, however, that you may "win the lottery" and get your first weekend choice. It's worth a try. Your application will cost $6.00 to apply and $15.00 per hiker that would be charged once you receive a permit date.[vii] Please understand that these fees may change season to season. The Forest Service's website should have the most updated fee rates.

THINGS YOU NEED TO KNOW BEFORE REQUESTING YOUR PERMIT DATE

Hiking Members

If you are considering taking your son(s) or daughter(s) on the hike, be responsible and make a good assessment of their maturity to determine whether you take them. By maturity, I mean do they continually demonstrate good common sense? The Mt. Whitney Trail will require a lot of stamina and good common sense in staying on the trail. There are pinnacles where I have observed people just sitting above a drop of several thousand feet. There are "windows" where the trail goes across a "bridge-like" section and no sides exist to the trail. Should one venture too close to the edge, trip or fall, it could be tens to hundreds of feet before they stop on a ledge or bottom. There are rocks to climb just off the trail that can position one for a terrible fall, breaking arms or legs. There are several streams to cross via rocks in the stream or walking atop a set of wooden timbers for many yards to cross a stream. In summation, if your child is very venturesome and doesn't always listen to you when you really need them to, you may not wish to take them on this hike. I have seen grade school-aged children hiking this trail and they did fine. The youngest person to hike Mt. Whitney in a day was Tyler Armstrong, seven years old. He made it to the summit in 7 hours 50 minutes and completed the whole hike in 17 hours. Tyler apparently was inspired to make the hike after watching the film, "Walking the Great Divide", according to his father[viii]. I know that I probably would not have felt comfortable with my child taking this hike until he or she was about twelve years old.

Night hiking and what you will see with a group

If you have friends or acquaintances that enjoy a vigorous hike, you may wish to see if they have an interest in this hike. If none of your friends seem to have any interest in doing this hike, you may seek out a hiking club to see if they have members that might be interested. Before you fill out your permit application, you will need to know how many hikers will be in your party. You may have up to 15 hikers in a group. The application will ask for the leader name and any alternative leaders should the leader not make the hike. It will be the leader's responsibility to physically pick up the permit in Lone Pine prior to the hike. If you apply for your application as one person then find others who want to join you, you may have difficulty getting permits for them. Remember, much of the prime hiking days will be filled when the Forest Service holds the lottery after March 15.

Once you determine the hiking members who want to accompany you on the hike, you will need to make sure they can take the time off work or school to make the hike. Even though I discuss making this hike in a day, I recommend making it a four day event; one day to travel; one day to acclimate; one day to hike; and one day to return home.

HIKING ALONE

If you can't find a friend or acquaintance to hike with you, what then? I made two trips to Mt. Whitney without a hiking partner. My first year, I started at the Whitney Portal at about midnight. There was a group of about fourteen people taking a group photo and just preparing to start out on their hike. I watched them head out and then made my own preparations, double-checking my equipment and using the bathroom for one last time. By the time I started out on the trail, it was about 12:30 AM, slightly after midnight. The group taking the photo was long gone.

I figured that I would probably catch up with them on the trail, so I headed out. After about 45 minutes, I came upon the group. I wasn't hiking at a particularly fast rate, but probably faster than I would have had I not seen them preparing to start. When I came upon the group from the rear, they all volunteered to let me pass. I declined and told them I would rather just follow their pace if they didn't mind. I was welcomed into to group and exchanged names as we walked. I stayed with that group all the way up the mountain and back down to the switchbacks. After that point, I soloed the remaining distance.

On my second hike, I did not see anyone in the parking lot at the Portal or anywhere. I looked up the mountain, seeking shining headlamps and could find none. Since I couldn't find company, I wasn't going to wait for someone to come along, so I headed up the mountain. I hiked solo all the way up the mountain past the Trail Crest. Just beyond Trail Crest is a junction. The John Muir Trail (JMT) goes down the mountain and the other path goes up to the Mt. Whitney summit. I found two hikers heading up the JMT and waited until they reached the junction. They had mistakenly taken the John Muir Trail instead of the Mt. Whitney Trail and were coming back. I joined them to hike up to the summit. Once arriving on the summit, they had a quick lunch and headed back down. I did run across them at Mirror Lake taking a break and joined them to finish the hike.

I believe you have three concerns in hiking Mt. Whitney alone. First is possibly meeting a black bear on your hike. If you are very small in stature, you may want to make sure that you join a group to help satisfy this concern or carry bear spray for comfort. Secondly, the possibility to lose the trail in a couple of areas does exist. Carrying a global positioning system (GPS) may help eliminate this concern. Thirdly, should you become injured on the trail; you would have to wait for other hikers for assistance. Traveling with company really helps to provide comfort and it is always interesting to me to meet new people. However, if you can't find people to join you on your hike, you may consider going alone. It is very common for small groups from one to three people to "latch" onto a group going from one rest stop to another. This takes place going up and down the mountain. It's almost like a small group catching a ride on a train, just from one stop to another. The hikers I have met are unbelievably friendly and have always welcomed anyone to join their hiking group. If the only way I could hike Mt. Whitney was with hiking partners or not going on my hike, I would have missed two hikes. I am glad that I decided to take my chances and travel to Mt. Whitney alone.

SCHEDULING YOUR TRIP

While you are trying to determine the best days to hike for your permit application, you need to know or determine the total number of days needed for the hike. Many people have to determine at least one day to get to Lone Pine, California. It is located on the eastern side of the Sierra Nevada Mountain Range, just off US 395, about one hour's drive south of Bishop, California. The closest airports to Lone Pine for the budget conscience are San Francisco (SFO), Oakland (OAK), Las Vegas (LAS), Ontario (ONT) or Los Angeles (LAX). These five airports should provide sufficient opportunity to look for specials according to your own closest airport. Once you arrive at one of these airports, you will still need to travel about five to seven hours to Lone Pine. If you are coming from the east coast, it may take you a full day of air travel to get to one of these airports and still have your five- to seven-hour drive to Lone Pine.

If you can get to Lone Pine by before 4:30 PM, you should be able to pick up your permit at the Visitor Center, located at the intersection of US Highway 395 and CA State Road 136. Their operating hours are from 8:00 AM to 5:00 PM, daily. [ix] At this point, your travel day planning consideration should be either one day if living in a day's drive of Lone Pine to two days if having to fly a long distance.

ACCLIMATION

If you were able to reach Lone Pine in sufficient time to stop by the US Forest Service Visitor Center (part of the U.S. Department of Agriculture), and obtain your permit at the end of your travel day, you can be ready to make a leisurely hike the following day to acclimate to the high altitude. If you had to arrive after the Visitor Center closed, you can pick up your permit in the morning after 8:00 AM.

Your acclimation day should begin with a good breakfast, packing up your hiking gear and driving to Whitney Portal. You will want to make a short two-hour hike to Lone Pine Lake. This site is a scenic lake overlooking the Owens' Valley. Your goal is to spend about two hours at the lake to acclimate. You will be at approximately 10,000 feet in elevation. Your hike would have begun from Mt. Whitney Portal with an elevation of 8,365.[x] It should take about 1 ½ hours to hike to Lone Pine Lake, so your total time above 8,000 feet should be approximately 5 hours. This time at high altitude will give your body an opportunity to start making its adjustments for the high altitude you will make on your hike.

Lone Pine Lake

Once you have completed the acclimation hike, you will want to get something to eat and begin preparing for your main hike. Your hike may begin as early as 10:30 PM that same day up to around 2:00 AM the following morning. Since you may begin soooooo early, you will probably want to get into bed about 4:00 PM to get some sleep.

THE HIKE

Whether you start later in the day of your acclimation hike or leisurely stay in bed until about midnight, you will want to get a very early start on your hike. Depending on your weather, physical preparation, number and length of rests and time on the summit, you may spend as much as 18 to 20 hours on the mountain. Your third day is filled with walking, viewing and resting. You should plan to finish your hike prior to sunset so you don't have to put your headlamps back on to finish your hike. The headlamps will not provide the best of vision for the descent as you will be tired and may not pick up on some rough spots in the trail which could cause you to trip and fall.

TRAVEL HOME

When you get back to the motel after your hike, you will definitely feel like getting something to eat and then getting some rest. This is NOT a good time to put others at risk and try to drive home after such as vigorous hike. It is too easy to fall asleep at the wheel and badly injure yourself as well as others on the road. You should definitely plan on traveling home the next day.

READY TO FILL OUT THE APPLICATION

This means for the sake of your travel planning, you would need one day to travel to Lone Pine if you live in or around California. Your acclimation hike day would be a second day. Your main hike would be a third. And, one more day to travel home would require a fourth day. If you are flying into one of the airports, you would want to add two more days to the four or six days. You will probably want to take a calendar and plug in the necessary days for travel and highlight the hike day. This would be the day or days you would want to enter on the permit application for your hike.

You should now have the information needed to fill out your permit application. You have knowledge of the weather and hiking conditions according to the months; you have a idea of how to get other hikers to join you in the adventure; you have an idea of the most popular times that others may apply for the limited permits and the days of the week that may land you a permit; lastly, you have an idea of the total travel and hiking time needed to pick your best dates for the application.

WHAT IF IT'S BEYOND MARCH 16 TO GET A HIKING PERMIT?

If it is beyond March 16 and the lottery has produced a goodly number of filled hiking dates on the calendar, there is still hope. You will need to be very flexible. Go to the RECREATION.GOV website and look for the calendar for available hiking dates, or call the USDA Forest Service in Bishop, (760) 873-2400, and see what dates are available.[xi]

The earlier in the year, the easier it should be to obtain a hiking date, but it may not be your most desirable time. For my first hike, the dates were largely full, but I still had several dates to pick from but all seemed to be mid-week.

MOTEL RESERVATIONS

Once you have obtained an acceptance for a permit, the most immediate following task is to make your motel reservation. Before calling or checking out the motels online, make a list of your motel requirements so you will be staying in the facilities that you need.

Lone Pine is the closest town to Mt. Whitney. There are other towns, Independence and Olancha that are just a few miles further out from Mt. Whitney and would require you to drive just a little further for your acclimation hike and main hike.

Remember that the Forest Service only allows 100 day hikers and 60 overnight campers per day. If you assume that all permits have been taken on and around your hiking date, which would be approximately 150 rooms to reserve around your hiking date for the other hikers. I allowed fifty percent to be double occupancy. You should also be aware that Lone Pine is one of the wider spots in the road for US 395, going up and down the Sierra spine of California. In 2012, I received my permit notification and checked availability of the motels. Just after checking, I sent an email to my friend, Ron Upson, who was planning on hiking with me. The next day, I tried to make my reservations and found that all the days I required for my hike were not available. There is a good selection of motels in town, but I learned to make my reservations right away if I want a specific motel.

In Lone Pine, there are several motels: two are national chains, Best Western and Comfort Inn. The Comfort Inn provides a refrigerator and microwave oven in the room. The Best Western has a refrigerator in the room: however, you would have to use the microwave oven in their breakfast room to warm or cook food. The other motels in town, Budget Inn, Dow Villa, Mt. Whitney Motel and Portal Motel offer refrigerators and microwave ovens in the room.[xii] The Lone Pine Chamber of Commerce website provides links to all the motels or phone numbers. They also include information on Independence and Olancha motels.

You will want to double-check the amenities of the motels and availability for your hiking date. Depending on what you want for a hiking breakfast, it may require either cooking or warming your breakfast. If you follow my suggestion for a very early start, you will be fixing breakfast in the late evening. Many of the restaurants will probably be closed by that time, except for possibly fast food restaurants. I suggest that you make sure when making your reservations that you have usage of a refrigerator for any food you brought for breakfast and a microwave oven to prepare it.

If you are hiking with or as a group, I suggest that you try and stay in the same motel. It allows you the comfortable opportunity to gather on the first travel day and cover the plans for the acclimation and main hike. If your group is assembling for the first time, there may be some surprises that need addressing.

In 2012, the group met for the first time after my arrival on my travel day. Several members of the group were not aware that the plan was to leave at 10:30 PM for our main hike. I had to make my case on the purpose of such an early time. We ended up settling on 11:00 PM departure from the hotel and were still late. The meeting is an excellent time to get everything on the table and discuss any concerns.

If everyone in the group is in the same motel, it is easy to meet and no one has to drive if the meeting is over cocktails. It is also easier on carpooling to Mt. Whitney.

DAY ONE – TRAVEL

The first day is a travel day. If you are coming in from the Midwest or East, you may have to plan an additional day due to flight connections. If you had a "magic wand", you would want to arrive before 4:00 PM to allow time to check into your motel and get to the USDA Visitor Center on the south end of Lone Pine and pick up your hiking permits. The time required to get your permit should be short unless there is an abnormal amount of visitors visiting the center at that time. Once you get to see a Forest Ranger at the desk, you can usually get all the paperwork done in about five to ten minutes. They will want your name, accompanying hikers' names, leader names, car license and have you sign some documents stating that you understand that you are NOT to keep food items or anything that looks to contain food, like coolers in your car. They will also want you to acknowledge that you are to carry out EVERYTHING that you take in. Afterward, they will give you a WAG BAG for each hiker. The WAG BAG is to carry your feces should you have to poop while on the mountain. You're then all set for your hike.

If you have to arrive after the visitor center closes, don't worry. Just get up early the next morning and get your permit as they open. Don't sleep in if you are doing your acclimation hike. You have a LONG day ahead.

If you are lucky enough to get to Lone Pine or your motel location in the early afternoon, you can do several things:

1. Go to the Movie Museum on the south side of town. It has a lot of memorabilia on movies shot in Lone Pine or the Alabama Hills. The Alabama Hills are on your way to Mt. Whitney. If you take the time to see the museum, you won't be disappointed. You'll

see old and newer movies shot here. Many of the motels have posted pictures of the past western stars that starred in roles here.

2. Go to the Alabama Hills, located west of town on Whitney Portal Road. You may recognize some of the backgrounds that you have seen in movies. It is interesting just to drive around and see what is there.

3. Go downtown and just tour the stores. There are several outdoor stores as well as restaurants to check out what you would like for dinner that evening.

4. Veg out at your motel. You will be very busy in the next few days. It's not a bad idea to just lay by the pool, if they have one, and relax.

5. Prepare to take some night photos. If you haven't practiced taking night sky photos, this is a perfect night to do so. With the dark skies of Lone Pine, you will probably have a ton of stars out in the evening and the ability to join terrestrial sights like trees to the skies. If you are looking across the freeway toward Mt. Whitney, some great images can be made with the streaking car lights looking slightly upward to the sky. It's all up to your imagination.

6. Have a pre-hike meeting, if you are in a group.

Get some good sleep after a good dinner and your evening activity. You should plan on a fairly early start on Day Two. This may be your acclimation hike. Day two and day three will seem to be one long day.

GROUPS, GROUP DYNAMICS AND PLAN-NING MEETING

If you are in a group or organizing a group, I suggest having a meeting at the end of your travel day to Lone Pine at place where you are staying. This meeting is to make sure everyone is aware of the need for an acclimation hike, what time to meet for the main hike, possible carpooling to the Portal, identify hiking partners, trail communications to signal the trail in confusion areas, bailout strategies and communication.

Groups and Group Dynamics

If you only have a small group of two or three, you may find it quite easy for everyone to stay up with each other or find a suitable hiking pace. When your group size gets above three, people begin to pair up into twos and threes. If your group has hiked together before, your hikers may know who likes to hike at his or her specific pace and who doesn't. It is important to match people up according to their pace. If a slower hiker is matched with a fast-paced hiker, pressure is put on the faster one to wait for the slower one, and the slower one feels pressure to hurry to stay with the faster one.

One needs to be able to hike at their preferred speed. If a hiker has to wait for a slower hiker, he or she may become chilled because he or she is not hiking at their comfortable pace to generate heat to keep him or her warm. Conversely, the slower hiker struggles to keep a pace of a faster hiker and does not get the adequate rests needed to help the body sustain the high-energy level needed for the long and strenuous hike.

In 2012, I was party to a group of five. Two people were traveling at a slower pace, a third traveling at a medium pace and one hiker liked to move at a fairly fast clip. As the group spread out due to the paces, I tried to have small rest periods at intervals to drink water, eat a snack and sit for a short minute or two. I found that as I waited for the slower couple to catch up, I was cooling down to a point that I became cold. When I started hiking again, I would heat up to a good comfort level. The slower pair worked hard to just make it to the resting period stop and the others were ready to move on. This didn't give the slower couple a chance to really rest and if the faster hikers stayed too long at rest, they became cold. Since the slower couple began to really push themselves to try and stay with the faster hikers, they eventually began to show signs of altitude sickness in the form of headaches. One of the hikers took several aspirin but even that didn't help as she ascended to the higher altitudes. Eventually, at about 12,000 feet, just shy of Trail Camp, the couple decided they needed to go back down. The headaches and cold had just become too much. Three of us in the group waited for them to arrive and a hiker came through telling us that the couple had turned back and asked the hiker to inform us.

This was the first hike for our group. All of us came from different areas of the west so there was no familiarity with each one's hiking pace preference. If you have a pre-hike meeting, matching up to hiking-pace preferences may greatly assist in getting the entire group to the summit. Your test run can be your acclimation hike. This would allow the subgroups the opportunity to feel out each other's pace and determine if they needed to make group changes.

Planning Meeting

If you have a planning meeting, it is a good time to relax and get to know one another. It is a great time to share hiking experiences and preferences. It would be ideal if everyone has previously hiked together but this may not be the case if you have assembled from different parts of the state, country or world.

During your meeting you should make sure that everyone is in agreement to your main hike start time. I found that my group in 2012 had no idea that I planned on starting at about 11:00 PM the day before our official hiking date. It took me a while to share the reasoning for an early start and get their buy-in.

Other issues to tackle are covering the need to hydrate and eat frequently on the hike. In 2012, one member was really slowing down. He was offered an energy packet and tried it. Afterwards he realized that he had been starving his body while constantly draining energy during the hike. He, then, began to eat on the breaks and claimed to have more energy as well as feeling better. You won't become thirsty and feel hunger pangs until you are well dehydrated or energy deprived. You will need to start drinking water at the outset of the hike and continue until you reach the Portal again. For energy, you will need to eat at EVERY stop to resupply your body's energy supply. If you wait until you're just too tired to continue, you may make a decision to abandon your hike to your disappointment later on because you didn't reach the summit.

Altitude sickness is a major issue on the hike. As I stated earlier, one member really began to experience bad headaches. She tried aspirin on several breaks but it did not seem to help. She was probably hiking too fast and gaining elevation faster than her body could adjust. After reaching about 12,000 feet, she just didn't feel well enough to continue. Descending is the right cure for the problem. It is possible that they could have gone to a lower altitude and remained for a while to acclimate. However, I think if the headaches are persistent, it is probably best to just get off the mountain. Altitude sickness can be deadly, so don't play with it.

It is important to make sure everyone has proper clothing for the hike. In the 2012 hike, we talked with several people who had made it to Trail Crest, 13,600 feet, and just couldn't continue because they were too cold. I attribute that to poor planning on proper clothing. Everyone should have sufficient layers of clothing to be able to start in the high 30s or low 40s at the outset of the hike. They should be able to put on layers when they begin to feel a chill. It will probably get windy at some part of the hike and everyone should be prepared to fend off the wind. I hiked Mt. Whitney three times previous to the 2012 hike. In each hike, the wind seemed to begin when reaching Trail Crest. This was because I had typically experienced an east/west wind. In 2012, the wind began at about 2:00 AM when we were just above Mirror Lake. The wind was a north/south wind. Since the mountain range lies north/south, we were experiencing the wind much earlier than I had on my previous hikes. Since the temperature was in the low 40s, the group was becoming intimidated that they would not be able to handle the expected colder temperatures at a high altitude. Oddly enough, when we reached the Trail Crest, the wind began to subside as it was about 9:00 AM. We reached the summit with one of the calmest (I probably should say less windy) and warmest days of reaching the summit I had experienced. One cannot assume that an early wind and cold morning will be unbearable on the summit. You have to get there to see what the weather will actually be like. Just plan to fend off the wind and have sufficient layers to keep you warm.

If the group is broken up into smaller groups that are more compatible in hiking paces, two items of communication need to be shared and understood . . . how to communicate the trail continuation when it appears to end and how to let others in the group know if you have decided to end your hike and descend the mountain.

There can be some areas of confusion where the trail crosses over large granite areas and any rock-lined paths will stop. In these areas, the group should agree on a method of signaling to the following group members where to pick up the path. This can be done by small rocks lined to show the direction to follow. If each subgroup has a GPS with them, most of the confusion should be a non-issue. However, when one begins to look for the trail and cannot find the continuation, it may take several minutes to walk around and look for the trail. A simple alignment of rocks in those areas can speed up the identification process and greatly assist your pals.

Lastly, each subgroup should realize that they should descend should they feel altitude sickness or they are just not going to be able to make the summit. After several hours of hiking, the distance between subgroups may be a mile or two. Each subgroup should not be waiting for others to arrive just so they can continue up the mountain. Every group member should have a cell phone with them. If a subgroup decides to descend, they should send a text message, voice mail and email to each member of the group. These messages should be sent upon the decision to descend. There are some cell phone hotspots on the mountain. During the descent, the messages will probably be sent. Albeit it may be a surprise to hear it suddenly sent. The message will probably not be received until a group gets back to the Portal but at least all groups that complete the hike will know who has decided to call it a day. Otherwise, the choice is to all, slowly hike the mountain or all take a roll call back at the motel. If someone has not descended, your group will want to know who it was and try to find out if they were in front of behind a subgroup. Don't wait until the next morning to find out who made it off the mountain and who might need help.

DAY TWO – ACCLIMATION HIKE

ACCLIMATION HIKE

If you follow my recommendation, you will actually start out on the day prior to your hike date on Mt. Whitney. This is the day you will hike to Lone Pine Lake to acclimate. There are other mountains on the way to Lone Pine where you can climb above 10,000 feet without having to obtain a hiking permit. I like the hike to Lone Pine Lake because it is a simple hike and is close to Lone Pine. You will get to see a portion of the hike in the daylight that you might not otherwise get to see in a fresh frame of mind.

From the town of Lone Pine, you will take Whitney Portal Road to Mt. Whitney.[xiii]After traveling through the Alabama Hills, they will look familiar if you have ever watched old western movies; you will arrive at the Whitney Portal after about a 20 minutes drive. There are a few switchbacks on the road but it is well maintained. You will find several parking lots and depending on the time of your arrival, you may have to park further down the road from the actual Portal. There is a store just above the Portal where you can buy some Mt. Whitney souvenirs or even a breakfast or sandwich. There are two toilets just outside the Portal should you need to go before heading up the mountain.

Mt. Whitney Portal

Wherever you choose to do your acclimation hike, this is a time to check out your GPS, your water sanitization, your camera, your food supply and your pace for the hike. If you are hiking to Lone Pine Lake, park your car in the parking lot, check your list for your backpack, trekking pole(s), ice axe and crampons (if you brought them), sun block, hat, and insect repellent. Omitting a comfort or aid at this point can carry over to your main hike and make it less enjoyable. For example, if you don't use the sun block, you could get a rather good sun burn or forgetting the insect repellent can give you some unplanned itches on your main hike.

Beginning of the Mt. Whitney Trail

Make your way from the parking lot to the trail-head. You WILL notice that you will get winded just walking to the Portal. This is the result of the altitude. You are about 8,365 feet[xiv] in elevation. As you start out on the trail, take some pictures and get an idea of the "lay of the land". In the darkness of an early start for the main hike, you will only see darkness and a small-lighted area wherever you look with your headlamp.

Start out at a fairly slow pace. You are not in a race and one of your goals should be to determine the hiking pace for the main hike. A slow pace provides more opportunity for your body to begin acclimating to this high altitude. If you are going up with friends, it is an excellent time just to have light conversation and see how the pace works for everyone. If you are going as a group, this is an excellent time to see how various hikers match up on preferred hiking paces. Many hikers appear to want to "run" up the mountain. These are the same people you may see on the main hike, totally spent and heading back down without reaching the summit.

Stream crossing with rocks (Lone Pine Creek North Fork)

You will initially start at a slight incline that follows a very clearly cut trail. You will be walking through vegetation. The trail will begin to have some cutbacks to change your direction on the ascent. Later, you will cross a small stream and then hear and sense that you are coming into an area of larger streams. The first stream is very small, just a few inches across. Stream by stream will get wider and wider. Eventually, you'll see that you have to cross over stepping stones. Just keep your balance and walk the stones. If you brought a trekking pole, you will find it quite helpful in crossing the stream. You will have more streams to cross, each one getting wider. Take mental notes of these streams since you will be crossing them again in the dark.

Stream crossing with timbers (almost at Lone Pine Lake Junction)

You will eventually reach a very wide stream that is adorned with square logging timbers. It is easy to walk but again, using the trekking pole helps to keep your balance. The main issue if you lose your footing is that you are going to get your feet wet. Hopefully, you have an extra pair of socks in your backpack for this situation. Otherwise, you may get some blistering on your feet due to chafing from your wet socks. If you also notice the amount of vegetation around the stream, you can plan on mosquitoes welcoming you to the area. Hopefully, you put on the insect repellent before you started along with the sun block.

After you cross the timbers, you are almost to the Lone Pine Lake Junction. The lake is down to your left. If you continue on, you will find a sign that informs you that you are entering the Inyo National Forest and permits are required beyond that point. Should you decide to ignore the post, you may be asked to leave and even receive a fine for hiking without a permit. The permit MUST be for the day you enter the hiking area.

Lone Pine Lake to your left is below the area requiring a permit. Walk down to the lake; it's maybe 100 yards. You will probably find some tents and campers located just along the lake. Take some pictures of the area and have a snack. It will take about 1 ½ hours to 2 hours to reach this point from the Portal.

Lone Pine Lake (9,938 feet)

You may see a large patch of snow just above the lake that continues around the surrounding area. If you brought an ice axe and crampons, this would be an excellent time to practice self-arresting and walking with crampons. There are several videos on self-arresting with an ice axe online on YouTube, http://www.youtube.com/watch?v=lm3xlshmnnk.[xv] The purpose of self-arresting is to right oneself should you fall or begin to slide on an icy slope. The chances are pretty good that you will find snow and ice somewhere on your hike the next day. For using crampons, check out http://www.timeoutdoors.com/expert-advice/walking-advice/winter-walking/how-to-use-crampons[xvi] I have hiked two times without an ice axe and took crampons for the first time in 2012. I found the ice axe to be a good accessory going through some of the snow fields above Mirror Lake and just below Trail Camp. The switchbacks may also have areas of ice and snow. In the early morning before sunrise, the ice is hard and not very penetrable with trekking poles. The ice axe cuts right through to give one a way to stop sliding or steady oneself walking through the snow. Crampons can be a huge help in walking through snow. Your time at Lone Pine Lake can also be used to practice putting on the crampons and using them to walk in the snow. Practicing putting the crampons on and taking them off will pay off on the Trail. You will have more confidence in using the crampons in a useful situation. Spend your time practicing with the crampons and ice axe.

Ice at Lone Pine Lake

After spending about one to two hours at Lone Pine Lake, it's time to head back down the mountain. Just take your time and notice the different muscles you are beginning to use on the descent. If you lengthen your trekking pole just slightly to help you take some of the stain off your knees, you will find descending much easier. This is especially true when you find yourself having to make larger step-downs from rocks onto the trail. The steps appear to be from eight inches to about twenty inches. The descent on the next day will be the toughest since you will have walked several miles to reach this point.

Once you have made your way down the trail and to your car, hopefully it is about noon or shortly after. Unloading your gear and driving back to Lone Pine should take about thirty minutes to an hour. It is time to have a good lunch or actually dinner when you get back to town. You will need to get an early start in just a few hours so you will need to get some rest.

MAIN HIKE PREPARATION

If you target a 9:00 PM or 10:00 PM departure from your motel, you don't have much time to get some sleep. Remember it takes approximately two hours to get to Lone Pine Lake Junction. You can technically enter the "permit zone" after midnight. This can be especially beneficial if the weather forecast is calling for thundershowers the next day. Typically, the thundershowers appear to begin just after noon. Targeting to reach the summit and start your descent by 11:30 AM is a good idea to avoid inclement weather. To meet this schedule, you may need to plan from six (for fast hikers) to about twelve hours (for slower hikers like me) and depending on your group size (larger groups tend to take longer breaks and hike at a slower pace). I have typically taken about eleven hours to reach the summit. My first year was the only time that I reached the summit with clouds gathering to the southwest. I reached the summit at about 11:30 AM and was headed back down just after noon. I just barely beat the snow that started to fall as I reached Trail Crest on that specific descent. In 2010, I reached the summit after about 9 ½ hours hiking, and in 2011, it took me 11 ½ hours. In both years it was not cloudy but the wind and cool temperatures were more than I wanted to remain on the summit very long. If you consider July as the pivotal hiking month, the closer to June will have more snow and closer to August less snow but more chances of afternoon thundershowers.

After you have lunch/dinner, check your packing list and make sure everything is packed for your hike. You may wish to load your car with everything except your backpack. You may want to fill the water bladder with ice so it will begin to melt while you take your "nap". I would recommend checking off each item to ensure you have everything. Know where all your items are and make sure you have a plan to get all the items into your backpack or trunk of the car. This is also a good time to make sure you have your breakfast items ready in your refrigerator. You are going to need a super breakfast to give you a great energetic start on the trail. Now, GET SOME SLEEP!

DAY THREE – MT. WHITNEY HIKE

Breakfast Time

Your alarm should go off in plenty of time to shower, refresh yourself and have a good breakfast. This is the MOST refreshed you will feel for some time. Now is also time to take a bathroom break to try and avoid having to go on the mountain. Remember, you have to bring out everything that you take in. It is also a good time to make sure your WAG BAG is in your backpack.

It's time for breakfast. I strongly feel breakfast is extremely important to make your Mt. Whitney hike a good experience. You will be expending a lot of energy in the next several hours and will need to amass a large number of calories for your hike. You should have plenty of carbohydrates and protein packed for your snacks and lunch. Breakfast should provide a good energetic start. Here is one recommendation (all items are preparation is determined for one person):

Huevos Marvos

Utensils needed:

1 plastic fork

1 plastic knife

1 plastic spoon

Paper ware:

1 paper bowl

1 paper plate

3 napkins, two for cooking and one to use for breakfast.

Food ingredients:

4 pieces of bacon OR 2 links of sausage

3 eggs

½ teaspoon white pepper

½ teaspoon minced dried onion

1 teaspoon minced Serrano peppers with seeds (if you want it less spicy, use jalapeño peppers or even bell peppers)

1 piece of sliced Swiss cheese

4 slices avocado

Preparation: Place bacon or sausage on paper plate, cover with napkin (absorbs the grease and prevents spattering the inside of the microwave). Microwave for 2 minutes, or cook to your desired doneness. Drain grease and put aside to enjoy with Huevos Marvos.

Add white pepper, minced dried onions and Serrano peppers (if you don't like spicy food, leave out the peppers) to a paper bowl. Add eggs and stir vigorously for about 25 strokes. Strip cheese into 1-inch sections and add to mixture. Microwave on high for 60 seconds. Take out mixture and cut up the egg that has solidified. Microwave the mixture for another 30 seconds. If the mixture is too wet to your liking, microwave for an additional 10-15 seconds. When cooked to your satisfaction, add slices of avocados on top.

This breakfast may sound rather spicy and it is, however, the avocado will act like a fire extinguisher if a bit is too hot for your taste. The bacon or sausage will provide the saltiness for the meal.

If you are preparing breakfast for a group, I suggest making each hiker a personal bowl to be cooked individually.

Enjoy your breakfast and take your last bathroom break before heading for Mt. Whitney. The time should be anywhere from 10:00 PM to 1:00 AM. If you are planning on a slow ascent get on the road around 10:00 PM. If you plan a faster ascent, you can leave later in accordance to your hiking plan. You may want to check the weather forecast one more time before getting on the road.

Leaving for Whitney Portal

Get your backpack and add ice in the water bladder to about fifty-percent capacity and then fill it with water. Load the food into your backpack in a location that is easy to constantly retrieve a snack. This is the time to apply your sun block and insect repellent and stow those items back into a place that can be easily accessed. Just for peace-of-mind, you may want to review your packing list one more time to mentally think through where everything is located. This is a great time to double-check where your headlamp is since it will provide your vision for the next several hours. Hop in your vehicle and head for Whitney Portal prepared for a fun but long day.

Whitney Portal Ready to Hike

Head up the mountain, find a parking place and get your equipment on. There are toilets for one last stop should someone need to go. A water fountain is just outside for washing hands. Gather with your group, wait for others to arrive and join them or get ready to head up by yourself. If you are with a group, this is the time to make sure everyone knows what to do if they reach their own personal limits. Is he or she to stay at that point until the others come back down; are they to meet at a certain rendezvous place? If everyone understands at this point, less confusion will happen on the trail. If anyone wants to take some aspirin or ibuprofen, this is a good time to do it. Remind everyone to begin drinking water almost immediately and suggest how long it will be to the first rest stop. You may wish to take a picture of the group at the Portal and even weigh the backpacks to know how much weight each person is carrying. It's time to head up!

Mt. Whitney Portal

If you are one who likes to have waypoints to know how far it is from one spot to the other, here is a listing for your own distance planning:

DISTANCE GUIDE

From	To	Distance
Whitney Portal	North Fork Lone Pine Creek	0.9 miles[xvii]
North Fork Lone Pine Creek	Lone Pine Lake Junction	1.9 miles[xviii]
Lone Pine Lake Junction	Outpost Camp	1.0 miles[xix]
Outpost Camp	Mirror Lake	0.5 miles[xx]
Mirror Lake	Trailside Meadows	0.8 miles[xxi]
Trailside Meadows	Trail Camp	1.0 miles[xxii]
Trail Camp	Trail Crest	2.2 miles[xxiii]
Trail Crest	"End of Pinnacles"	1.2 miles[xxiv]
"End of Pinnacles"	Mt. Whitney Summit	1.0 miles[xxv]
Total Whitney Portal	**Mt. Whitney Summit**	**10.5 miles**

MT. WHITNEY TRAIL

MT. WHITNEY PORTAL (8.365 feet)[xxvi]

As you start out on the Mt. Whitney Trail, you will pass through an actual Portal which looks like an actual gateway to the mountain. There is a scale at the Portal so you may weigh your backpack just to see how heavy it is at the onset of your trek.

To give you an overview of the Trail, think of a large granite mountainside that has some lakes positioned on the mountain at the mid elevations. These lakes are formed from ice and snow melting. As the lake fills and starts to send water down the mountain from an overflow, the streams will have vegetation growing on the stream sides for several hundred yards. Once the vegetation ends due to its far proximity from the water, you will see mostly rock and granite faces. Once above the tree line, there is actually no brush and only rock. If you want to average the total hike, it will be a 9% incline for about 10.5 miles uphill and a 9% decline for about 10.5 miles downhill.

The Mt. Whitney Trail, itself, is actually a gentle slope that follows the water trails from the higher lakes. The last lake at Trail Camp will have a steeper slope that is lessened via switchbacks and actually called the Switch-backs. The top of the Trail crosses over to the backside of the mountain ridge face. From that point, the Trail heads north toward Mt. Whitney and will summit from the west side of the ridge.

The Trail begins as a rock-lined path and is quite easy to follow. You will see brush growing above and below the trail. The Trail will continue to the north until it makes the first switchback. If you look at the map, you will see that the Trail is actually quite a round-about-way for the first mile just to give you an easy walk. There is another trail from the parking lot that is more direct but a steeper trail.[xxvii] After the first switchback, you will begin to hike in a more normally straight path to the top of the ridge. You will begin crossing some very small streams. One after another, they seem to get wider. You will then begin to find streams that require walking and balancing on stones to cross. These, too, seem to get wider and wider until you meet a very wide stream that has log cross beams laid to give you a dry passage through the creek. At this point, you are very close to Lone Pine Lake Junction. Lone Pine Junction is a fork to either head back down the mountain slightly to Lone Pine Lake or to continue on the Trail to Mt. Whitney.

LONE PINE LAKE (9,938 feet)[xxviii]

Lone Pine Lake Junction is at an elevation of approximately 10,030 feet[xxix] Lone Pine Lake is located about 100 feet below the junction. It is a beautiful lake that faces Owens Valley. It takes somewhere from 1 ½ hours to 2 hours to reach this point from the Portal at a nice leisurely pace.

Should you decide simply to continue on from Lone Pine Lake Junction, you will see a sign that informs you that you must have a permit to proceed on. The trees are starting to thin out and the brush is getting more sparse.

Above Lone Pine Lake Junction you will begin some switchbacks through a rocky path that takes you to a stream requiring a stepping stone crossing. You are then at Outpost Camp.

OUTPOST CAMP (10,365 feet)

Outpost Camp is a very flat area sparsely enclosed by trees. You will probably see some campers here. It looks like a typical camp ground you would expect in Yosemite or other national parks. Your elevation at this point is approximately 10,365 feet.[xxx]You will have about a 150 yard to 200 yard walk through this area to reach another stream crossing and switchback section that will take you to Mirror Lake.

MIRROR LAKE (10,670 feet)[xxxi]

Mirror Lake

As you travel upward toward Mirror Lake, you will hear the stream along the trail. You will see more brush along the trail and probably find more mosquitoes to welcome you as you near Mirror Lake. There will not be any campers around as they are not allowed to camp in this area. You will walk along the lake for a while and then start up into some trees and rocks. After a little climb, you will find a large granite area where the trail will disappear since you are walking on a huge rock. You may have to look hard to find the continuation of the Trail but it is there. As you continue to climb, you will find yourself at Trailside Meadows.

TRAILSIDE MEADOWS (11,420 feet)[xxxii]

Trailside Meadows

At Trailside Meadows, you will see plenty of under-brush and vegetation. It is almost like walking by Mirror Lake but much longer. You will hear a stream or flowing water. This will last for quite a while. Again, you will start to climb through rock. If you are worried about meeting bears or mountain lions, you are leaving their normal area of habitation. From here on, you should expect to see mainly ground squirrels, chipmunks, mice and marmots. Above this area, the vegetation will become so sparse that bears will not normally reside. Depending on the number of rest stops you have made, you are somewhere in the vicinity of 3 to 4 hours into your hike.

Day break below Trail Camp

You are now traveling through on rocky surfaces. There is no vegetation around. As you walk, you will see a lake off to your left, this is Consultation Lake. You may find some campers near the lake but the lake is off your path. You will continue to travel upward through the rocks until you reach Trail Camp.

Lake at Trail Camp

Trail Camp usually has some tents strewn around. It is the last place you can get water from a lake. There will be one last chance for water as you continue up on the Switchbacks. Just consider that this water follows the Trail and you will be actually walking right through this water flow. You will want to make up your mind whether you want water from a lake or from an area people are constantly walking through.

The lake at Trail Camp will probably be covered with ice in the early morning and will melt as the day progresses. You will still need to either filter the water or sanitize the water via tablets or ultraviolet light. You should be running fairly low on water if you have been sipping sufficient water on your hike up the mountain. I usually find that I will consume almost 3 liters of water to this point.

Since this is the last source of water until you reach this area again after reaching the summit, you may wish to rest and refill here. You will need at least 3 liters of water to reach the summit and return to Trail Camp, or about 8.8 miles.[xxxiv] Most of this distance will be above 13,000 feet requiring even more water than you have used at the lower elevations. Incidentally, in 2012, I actually used up my 3 liters of water upon reaching the summit. I used my spare liter to keep me hydrated on the way back down to Trail Camp. While you resupply your water, it is a good time to also rest your feet by putting them above the rest of your body. It will provide some great comfort for a few minutes that you take in the rest.

Once you have rested and incidentally, this is one of the last places that should you need to take a restroom stop, it is a great place to go. Above this point, you will only be able to get slightly off the trail to use the bathroom. You will have hikers going by like a well-traveled two-lane highway.

The "Cables"

Just a couple of hundred yards from the lake at Trail Camp, you will begin the switchbacks. You will climb 1,325 feet in elevation but through a myriad of switchbacks on the trail. In the early morning, the trail will be covered with ice from the stream passing through the path.

Water on the Switchback Trail

Depending on the season, you may find small snow patches on the trail causing you to either walk on the snow or just above the trail to stay on the rocky surface. When you are about half-way, you will enter the cables. This is an area on the extreme right side of the trail where metal posts are sunk into the rock. Cables are strung from one post to another to provide a handrail against a steeper drop off from the trail. Again, depending on the season and snowfall, you may experience snow on the trail around the cables, causing you to walk above the trail to get out of the snow or work your way through the snow trail. If there has been a great abundance of snow prior to your hike, it is possible that you may wish to evaluate hiking up the chute which is just to the right of the switchbacks. It is a more direct route, but this would require hiking with an ice axe and crampons. To get back down through this area, glissading may be the main mode of descent.

The switchbacks will seem to go on forever. You will just reach one end of the incline and start right back in the other direction, making a slight elevation change. You will have some beautiful views from the switchbacks as you can see the whole mountain face or cliff all the way over to Mt. Whitney. After step after, never-ending step, you will eventually see the top of the crest coming into view. As you look back, you will see Trail Camp and Consultation Lake. As you look toward Mt. Whitney, you will see Boy Scout Lake and Iceberg Lake at the foot of Mt. Whitney.

Marv at Trail Crest

The switchbacks DO end and you will see a sign indicating Trail Crest. This is a good rest stop and great place to take photos of yourself and those traveling with you. Once you cross from the switchbacks and Trail Crest, you will walk over a slight window or area where there is a stone bridge from Trail Crest to the backside of the mountain ridge.

Guitar Lake on the backside of Trail Crest

You will start going downhill for a short distance. At this point, you will see the backside valleys and lakes. It is almost like another world. You should notice the wind picks up at this point since you will probably get an easterly or westerly wind. Once behind the rocks heading down the trail, the wind should subside. If you haven't donned more clothing up to this point, you will probably start thinking about it. The temperature will possibly be the coldest that you have experienced thus far on the hike. Coupled with the wind, you may wish to don a windbreaker or rain suit top to cut the wind and keep some of your body temperature.

Trail on the Backside of the Mountain to Mt. Whitney

The picture above shows the rough trail to follow and the ever-presence of the Mt. Whitney peak in the background. You are 2 ½ miles from the Trail Crest and about 2 miles from this picture's location. The closer you get to the summit, the more encouragement you will receive from those coming back down.

MT. WHITNEY SUMMIT (14,505 feet)xxxvi

The Summit to the East

The Summit to the West

After a short descent, you will be climbing down rocks; you will find a junction on the Trail. To the left, going downhill is Muir Trail and going to the right or up is the Mt. Whitney Trail. Stay to the right. At this point, the downhill hiking is now starting to go back up. If you look far in front of you, you will see the jagged mountain ridge line that begins to make a slight left or westward turn. This is Mt. Whitney. It looks a long way away and it is! You are somewhere between one and two and one-half hours from the summit, depending on how many stops you make and how you stand up to the altitude.

Trail across a "window"

This portion of the hike seems to go on forever, because you are anxious to get to the summit and you keep seeing pinnacles that look like they could be the Keeler Needle, the peak just to the south of Mt. Whitney. You will be stepping from one large rock to the other on most of the backside passage. When you reach an area between peaks, you will cross a window. The window is similar to the crossing from Trail Crest. There is a stone bridge between the peaks and if one trips and falls, it could be a ways before stopping the downhill slide. If you have a fear of heights, these areas will not be your favorite. Just keep your eyes straight ahead to the end of the window and walk. You'll be fine. The path has plenty of width to cause too much concern but visually, it may seem quite narrow. Most windows are about five to eight feet across. One point of caution, beware of sudden gusts of wind when crossing a window. If the winds are coming from either the east or west, you may lose a hat or cap from a sudden gust.

*View from a Window looking At Consultation Lake
in the distance*

You have hiked and hiked for about three miles and wonder if you will ever reach the top. Finally, you will see what may be a trail through a snow patch. You are really close to the summit! After crossing through the snow field you will see a small stone hut. This is the Smithsonian Hut, built in 1909. Just to the east of the hut, you have finally reached the highest point. You have been hiking between seven and maybe eleven hours to get here. The view is amazing! You can truly take a 360 degree shot of the vista since NOTHING else is in your way. You are at the highest point in the contiguous United States! CONGRATULA-TIONS! Feel good about your accomplishment and cherish the time on TOP! Try to get everything done on your summit list!

SUGGESTIONS FOR THE SUMMIT

After many hours of hiking, you reach the summit and now what? Do you just turn around and go back down? There are some opportunities on the summit that you will want to use to your advantage. This may be the only time in your life that you will be here. Plan in advance what you want to do and do it.

Pay Attention to the Weather!

Snow clouds on the horizon, time to start down off the summit

Even if you are reaching the summit early in the morning, keep an eye on all sides of the mountain for incoming weather. You may have planned to arrive early and get off the summit before typical storms tend to form, but bad weather can start ANY time. You should be able to see dark clouds at quite a distance and be able to respond by descending in a timely fashion. If you have been delayed on summiting or are "later" than expected, use good common sense on whether you should continue on to the top. Do NOT wait out a storm in the hut! That actually was the location of the first recorded death on Mt. Whitney from lightning.*xxxvii* If the storm clouds are gathering, get off the summit to a lower elevation that will be safer from lightning. If you're not seeing weather signs to cause concern, have some fun!

Sign the Log

Visitor Log at the Smithsonian Hut

One of the first things to do when you reach the summit is to sign the log in front of the Smithsonian Hut. You will see a metal covered table. Open the top and inside is a log for visitors to sign. Don't just sign the log; take a picture of your signature. I was told by a Forest Ranger that the log sheets go to the University of California, Berkeley. He did not know what they did with the logs. Who knows, you may be able to find your proof of ascent online at some future date, but for now, a picture will provide that proof to your friends and give you some good memories later on when you see the photo.

Take Panorama Pictures from the Summit

Panorama of the summit

You have no obstruction of a full, 360-degree series of photographs on the summit. There are actually apps for smart phones that piece together your various pictures to form one, continuous vista shot. Photoshop also offers a means to merge your photos into a panorama photo. If your camera is six megapixels or better, you will be amazed as to the detail and clarity of your photos.

If you just take a few minutes to look around, you will see the gentle western slope. As you look north and south, you will see the high peaks composing the Pacific Crest Trail. As you look to the east, you will see the Owens Valley some 10,000 feet below you. You will see lakes to the east and west. This is a time to take more photographs than you can ever use. You are just looking for a few good ones out of maybe fifty or sixty to honor your ascent.

Take Videos of Yourself on the Summit

Most digital cameras today have a video selection to allow you to take short video clips. This is an excellent time to record your feeling and excitement for posterity or to Tweet or post on Facebook. You can also pan the summit to show your friends and family what you saw, hear the wind and if you're moving around, hear you breathe rather hard.

Have Lunch

You have just hiked from six to twelve hours (six *for those of you who won the race up the mountain)*. You should have packed a REWARD for this accomplishment, lunch. Your lunch should be something that you enjoy but different from what you were eating on the trail to the summit. Make it special! Of all the people who started out the day, many will not make it to the summit. It may be from lack of preparation, altitude sickness (AMS), accidents, or whatever reason. You deserve something special that will also help provide fuel for you to get back down the mountain!

Get Warm

You will find the summit can be VERY, VERY cold. You are at the highest point in the contiguous United States. There is nothing around to shelter you from the wind at 14,505 feet in elevation; nothing to warm you except the sun. Once on the summit, your slow down of body movement will cause you to cool down. Be aware of how you are feeling. The Smithsonian Hut can provide the shelter you need to allow yourself time to warm up, eat lunch and get ready for your descent.

Change Your Socks

Now that you have come almost 11 miles, your feet are tired. This is an excellent time to change your socks. Dry clean socks will give you relief that you haven't anticipated. While you rest, prop your feet up to get them ready for the 11 mile descent.

76

Stick Your Head in the Smithsonian Hut

The Smithsonian Hut was built in 1909. It is over 100 years old. You have the opportunity to go inside the hut and just see it. There is nothing inside but an empty room, but it is still an artifact and it is an excellent wind-break. After relaxing a few minutes, your body will begin to cool and if the wind is REALLY blowing, you're going to get REALLY cold. The hut can be a great haven.

Geocaching

If you like Geocaching, there is a cache located at the summit for several years. Hopefully, you brought something to trade should you decide to find it and take an item. The general rule is to leave something of equal or more value for the next visitor. To learn more about Geo-caching, visit http://www.geocaching.com. Here you can learn the principle concept and rules of the game.

Hopefully you were prepared for the summit and took full advantage of everything it has to offer.

THE DESCENT

Now that you have reached the summit, given high-fives to those at the top, and rested a bit; you are ready to start back down. It won't take you as long to descend as it did climbing but the parking lot is still a long way away!

Now is the time to put on your thinking cap and stay awake, aware and attuned to your body, your environment and the weather. As you start back down, it will seem like only a short time before you reach the Trail Crest. You will find renewed energy as you start back down. Your body will almost sense invigoration. Because it seems so much easier to descend, it is easy to start making mistakes. Your body will be tired. You have probably used between 4,000 and 6,000 calories to make the summit. Hopefully, you were eating quite well and drinking plenty of water on the ascent. You still need to maintain the calorie intake on the way down.

After you reach Trail Crest, you will begin a much easier trip through the switchbacks. The snow will have softened and become quite slushy. Any ice you encountered on the way up is now a flowing stream of water. You will still need to be careful around the cables to keep good footing if it is a snow-covered trail at that point. Hikers before you have already made the paths to follow in most places. Here again, just use good common sense and make sure your footing is good and you don't get in too much of a hurry.

Ron Upson at cables with Trail Camp and Consultation Lake in the background

Each switchback will look upon Trail Camp and the lake below. You will get closer and closer. Finally, you will find yourself back at Trail Camp and this is a marvelous place to refresh your water supply and don the sun block and insect repellant as well as a short rest.

After your rest at Trail Camp, it is down, down, down on rock, rock, rock, rock. You will pass Consultation Lake and then have to work through a trail that seems to disappear. You will have walked on a granite area for quite a while and now you have to determine where the trail goes. If you used your GPS on the way up, you should have good direction on where to pick up the trail. You will continue on down to Trailside Meadows. By now the temperature has warmed and the mosquitoes received advance notice you were coming. They can be relentless. You are starting to get back into the areas where the streams flow and help vegetation grow. All this area will seem new if you had an early start because this is the area that was dark when you hiked by headlamp earlier in the morning.

Stream crossing on stones

After making your way through Trailside Meadows, you will finally descend into Mirror Lake. You are only about one and one-half hours to two hours from completing your journey! After all you have been through for the day; this will seem to be the most never-ending portion of the hike. You will be crossing streams, stepping down from stone after stone and walking down trails. Don't be surprised if you hear your smart phone pick up some emails or even receive a phone call, you will begin to hit some hotspots of cell coverage. Just remember that you may lose that coverage as suddenly as you became aware that you were in range. Eventually, you will reach the first bit of switchback you made at the onset of your hike. You are only about fifteen minutes away. Step after step, you finally see the parking lot and the Whitney Portal. Congratulations you made an awesome trip!

THE EXPERIENCE – WHAT IT FEELS LIKE

As you think about hiking about 22 miles and making an elevation climb and descent of 6,140 feet[xxxviii] in some 12 to 20 hours, you must wonder if this hike can truly be worth it. I admit training isn't fun. It is monotonous at times and one has to keep training when he or she really doesn't want to. However, this adventure provides many pluses you haven't anticipated.

First, the social interaction between you and your hiking buddies can be fantastic. You will learn a great many things about people you may barely have known before. If you end up hiking solo, you have an opportunity to catch up with some small group and hike with them. You may start some long-distance relationships with people that live in a totally different part of the country or world. As you start hiking with others, you will, of course, begin with small talk but the various subjects that come up during the hike will amaze you. It may be from things you see on the hike to discussing similarities or differences in families. By the time you finish, you will feel that you know your hiking buddy(s) quite well.

Rest Stop in the Dark

Your initial hike will probably start either late evening the night before your actual hike date or very early in the morning of your hike date. You will hear sounds of water flowing at times but you are mainly going to see the light shining on the trail in front of you for several hours. This does have an advantage on your descent. You won't recognize much of the lower Trail and all the beauty around it since you hiked this portion in the dark. You will be amazed at the scenery as you finish the last few hours of your hike.

Secondly, self-interaction can be extremely interesting. You have many, many hours to think, think and think. Even traveling with a group, the high altitude will help everyone to stay quiet and just hike. During these periods of silence, you will have time to self-reflect and think of many things that come to mind. I found this to be one of the most rewarding parts of hiking Mt. Whitney. I can't tell you how many of the world's problems I was able to solve. The only problem was I couldn't remember the genius answers to the problems at the end of the hike. I guess I'd better take notes next time.

Thirdly, the terrain is amazing. You will see vistas, birds, plants and varmints that you may not have ever seen. It is fun to watch the animals or just see them. As you climb higher and higher, your scenery changes quite drastically. You will see the backside of Mt. Whitney and the many lakes and valleys back toward Fresno. As you look back from the area you just came from, you will see a valley floor that is about 10,000 feet below you. You may experience forty-degree temperatures and down in the valley below it may be well over 100 degrees.

Fourthly, once you reach the summit, you have accomplished a goal that you planned to achieve for months. There is the guest sheet located just outside the Smithsonian Hut. Here you will sign in to provide official record that you accomplished your feat. This is a euphoric time. You can join in with the others giving "high-fives" for reaching the top.

There are many rewards for making this trek. There are social benefits, personal benefits with meeting new people and learning a new area of the country. It is also rewarding to reach the highest point in the contiguous United States. You will be tired the day following the hike but you will always have the "badge" that you reached a very high summit.

DAY FOUR – TRAVEL HOME

You've had quite an experience for the past two days. Hopefully, you listened to stay the third night and get some rest. I can't communicate to you just how you will feel, but I don't think I am far off from saying you will feel like you're 100 years old. Walking stairs, getting in and out of a car is real torture. The more you move the better you will begin to feel. Your muscles have been through a lot in the last two days. You hiked somewhere around 25 miles, starved your body from oxygen and tried to keep it hydrated with water and nourished with food. All those muscles that were used to just a few hours of usage were tested to the extreme. You have a right to feel old.

If you have a flight to catch, you may have to set your alarm to get you on the road early. If not, this is a great day to rest a little longer in bed and get ready to travel home. Give yourself time to make it back home or to your airport. You will be tired but it may be nice to plan a breakfast or lunch stop on your way home or to the airport.

If you have more time before having to get back, you are at the gateway to Death Valley. It may be a little warm, depending on the time of year, but it is a great visit. It provides you who like to participate in extremes, the opportunity to hike the highest mountain in the contiguous U.S. and reach the lowest point in the U.S. on the following day, making a total elevation change of 14,787 feet in just two days. Badwater is the lowest point at -282 feet below sea level.[xxxix]

BEGINNING INITIAL PREPARATION

If you're sold on making the hike, just where do you start and what is involved?

I believe that you should first check to determine if you will be able to make the hike THIS year. As initially mentioned, hiking Mt. Whitney is by permit only. If you are too far into the year and all the spots have been taken, are you willing to chance getting a spot where someone else over-estimated their party size and gave back some permits to the Forest Service? I would suggest calling the Inyo Forest Service (760) 873-2400[x1] to get their advice on obtaining a permit. If you don't live in close proximity to Mt. Whitney, you will have to travel and get motel accommodations. If you are determined to go, excellent! I wish you great luck and hope you are able to make it. You typically will find a short line in front of the Lone Pine Inyo National Forest Visitor Center each morning looking for hiking permits.

If the timing is on your side when looking at the lottery open dates and you see a vacancy on the website, grab it! It's $6.00 for the reservation and $15.00 per person for the permit. If you somehow can't go, it was a good donation to the Forest Service. While getting your permit, are you taking some friends or are you going by yourself? You'll need to make the call on how many permits you need.

Once you have your permit reservation, you are ready to proceed in gathering your necessary equipment and begin preparing physically for the hike. Oh yes, don't forget to get your motel reservation. You will want to get to Lone Pine, acclimate, hike and rest before returning home. That may take at least three evenings at the motel, perhaps more if you're coming from out-of-state.

If you want to take others on the hike, have you discussed it with them? The first three years of hiking the mountain, I was able to find hiking partner once. The fourth year, I was lucky because Ron Upson wanted to hike the mountain to honor his deceased friend, Chris Meining. Most people just hear about the physical preparation or actually energy exertion and don't want to go. If you are a member of a hiking club or have an adventurous friend(s), great! Sign them up!

You've decided to go arranged for your permit(s). Next you'll want to begin gathering your equipment and planning your training for your hike. You may wish to plan on three months preparation before the hike, but you can do it with much less. Just remember, even with good con ditioning, you will probably feel like you are 100 years old at the end of the hike. The difference in conditioning will determine HOW old you will actually feel after the hike. Is it 100 years old or 85? You're going to feel some aging here so get ready.

PHYSICAL PREPARATION

Your first couple of miles will be step after step after step. You will have to cross a few streams via rocks and then a long run of wooden ties. Later, you will start to climb step after step. Continuing on, you will find some good-sized steps where you have to climb around 30 inches or more on a step. Then later, it is several long steps then back to smaller steps. On the switchbacks, you will vary from walking over icy-water flow on the path to some good stretch climbs over rocks to make it to the cables. Once over the Trail Crest, you will go down and up over rocks for about 3 miles. This is a description of your hike on Mt. Whitney for six to eleven hours just to get to the summit. As you have been climbing most of the way, there are some short downhill strolls during the ascent. As you remember, what goes up must come down. Now you need to think about four to eight hours of a descent, using muscles that you didn't use on the way up. You will be lowering yourself down to rocks and the trail in quite a different manner than climbing. Just small steps from 8 to 12 inches will become a major chore on the way down toward the finish.

Stationary Bike or Spinning

The stationary bike can provide excellent muscle training for your legs. If you have one or access to one, it will help you greatly. The bike in the seated position forces you to use your legs in a climbing situation. It also provides excellent stamina training for extended periods of time. You should bike for about one hour per day, four days per week, in the 60 days prior to making your hike.

If you have a spinning class available to you, this is also excellent. The spinning class uses stationary bikes but with a trainer. The trainer usually has music to provide a cadence to peddle by. They typically have interval training which provides fast and slow speed peddling as well as hill climbing. This type of training increases the friction on the bike wheel to make it more difficult to spin. After about 50 to 60 minutes, you should be sweating quite well and pretty well energy-spent. I typically enjoy a spinning class two days per week. The time seems to pass by much more quickly in the spinning class since it is instructed and the peddling is paced to the music.

Stair Climbing

A stair climbing machine is an excellent means to deliver the rock climbing sensation that you will experience. I have seen two machines that produce this effect. One has two foot-peddles that go up and down with various resistances to provide the exercise. The other looks like a staircase that moves like an escalator. In either case, they provide the climbing simulation to help strengthen your leg muscles to make the climbs up and over rocks. If you can work on such machines two to three hours per week, you will appreciate the benefit at the end of your Mt. Whitney hike.

Inclined Treadmill

The inclined treadmill is a treadmill that will go beyond the normal 15-degree ascent offered by most treadmills. However, if you don't have one available, the 15-degree will do. Inclined treadmills will go as high as 30 to 50 degree inclines. This can be extremely helpful in training your muscles to make the ascent. Your main goal is to use the treadmill without holding onto the bars. That is a good goal but sometimes not practical if you just finished an hour on the bike. You may stabilize yourself by putting minimum pressure on the rails to keep your balance but avoid putting too much weight on the bars to relieve your exercise. You should use this machine about five days per week for one hour sessions (if you can spare the time). It will give your leg muscles the strength and stamina they need for the continuous climbing. If you listen to music while walking, try to find the beat of the music and stay with it. As your songs change, change your cadence. This means some songs will require a long stride and others a quick step. Your body needs those changes to properly develop the muscles.

Now is the biggest issue in preparation. Most treadmills are designed to provide strength for climbing but few provide the ability to decline it to a negative hike for the descent. You will find that you feel fine at the summit. No problem in the descent, right? Well, if all of your training has been devoted to the ascent, you are in for a RUDE surprise, the descent is what make you feel sooooooooooooo old the next day! You will even find yourself mumbling about little steps toward the end of the hike as you step over the smallest of rocks.

Some incline treadmills offer a negative degree of training. This may vary from -3-degrees to -5-degrees. My suggestion is to use this even for just a minimum of 5 minutes per inclined treadmill training. On your way down from the summit, you will appreciate this typically unused setting on the treadmill. As you get closer to your hike date, I suggest finding stairs or hills around you that will give you some long downhill training. At least the two weeks prior to your hike should be highly focused on building your muscles around your shins and sides of the thighs.

Outside Training

If you don't belong to a gym or health club or don't want to buy exercise equipment for your home, the outdoors provides a gym for you if you're willing to use it. This means using it in rain, shine, dark, wind, snow, or whatever the elements throw at you. Find yourself a location that has steps. It may be a courthouse, office building, school, or any place with a change in elevation. You can receive the necessary muscle training from just climbing steps. You should still plan on taking about ONE HOUR each week to walk the steps. Again, if you listen to music, change your cadence to stay in step with the music when possible.

Do you have a bicycle? It's time to use it. However, most of us will coast on the street when possible. Your charge is to constantly be peddling; this means taking a route that will keep you engaged in climbing or constantly peddling to keep a good pace on the road. Three to four days per week and covering about 20+ miles per day will do the trick, depending on the hilliness of where you live.

As a last recommendation, I offer "squat walks". A "squat-walk" is walking in a very slow fashion; taking your knee almost to the floor and then rising back up. The next step is taking the other knee almost to the floor and rising again. About ½ mile of this walk with your normal walking or running each day would give you the extra muscle training for those high climbs on rocks that are higher than 18 to 20 inches.

The amount of time you select to spend on training per day is yours to decide. You can always just go on the hike. The less training you do, the more repercussion you will have after the hike. Your body will help you during the hike, especially if you give it rest and feed it continually with food and water. You will accomplish your goal of hiking Mt. Whitney. The whole issue in training is how tired and sore you will feel after the hike. Believe me, after finishing the hike, even climbing or descending stairs or getting in or out of a car can become a major challenge. Your muscles will give you a payback for any lack of training!

You will need one month of training at the BARE minimum! I would suggest at least three months. Once I started training, I enjoyed the hike so much that I have continued my training year after year. When I take a break because of schedule changes for vacation or whatever reason, I find that I "pay" for the time off. Fitness is not just given to us. We must EARN it day after day. You can have some days off but there is a payback. Don't relax too many days before getting back into the routine!

Bowel Training

I want to remind you that on this hike, you have plenty of cover for taking a bathroom break with privacy on the first four miles of the hike. After that, if you are modest, you will need to find some distance between hikers to relieve yourself. Yes, that is just talking about urinating. This hike is in the Inyo National Forest. Their rules state that you will bring out everything that you brought in. This includes feces. Part of the $15.00 fee includes a "Wag Bag" that is a plastic cloth to be laid down on the ground so you can take a "dump." There is toilet paper in the package. After defecating on the pad, you are to sprinkle the included powder and wrap up the "package". The idea is to put this bundle either hanging or attached to the back of your backpack until you have finished your hike, depositing it in a waste basket at the Whitney Portal. The MAIN issue is to not leave it on the mountain.[xli]

As you think through this process, you aren't too excited? This is not negotiable. You could receive a fine if you decide to disregard the rules. Even worse is other members of your party may not appreciate your disdain for nature. One of the advantages of doing the ONE-DAY hike is to resolve this concern. You have plenty of time to train your body into a regimented time for your bathroom breaks. I use Metamucil three times daily to keep me regular. In the four hikes I have done thus far, I have yet to have an urge to go while hiking the mountain.

Dehydration

High-altitude hiking requires constant hydration to keep the body functioning. One can hydrate by drinking water from bottles or using a hydration backpack. If you choose to use the water bottles, you will probably spend a lot of time taking frequent rests to drink your water. It is difficult to hike and drink water out of a bottle at the same time because of your need for oxygen. You will find that you will be breathing rather hard most of the way up the mountain. Just a simple slow-step pace at high altitude above 8,000 feet will require the same gasping as a good RUN at sea level. The hydration backpacks have a tube that one can easily put into his/her mouth and take a sip of water from the reservoir.

Altitude Sickness

Altitude sickness and dehydration may be closely linked. Altitude sickness can show itself in altitudes above 8,000 feet. Dehydration is simply losing more fluid than one takes in. The bodily fluids perform many functions including delivering oxygen, nourishment and helping the body dispose its constant collection of waste. When one ventures into the realm of high altitude, the amount of oxygen received from each breath is greatly reduced. One breathes more rapidly and with dryer air at high altitudes, the body rapidly dehydrates. Symptoms of altitude sickness include: difficulty sleeping, dizziness, fatigue and headache, loss of appetite, nausea, rapid pulse and shortness of breath. Extreme altitude sickness include: bluish discoloration, chest tightness, confusion, coughing, decreased consciousness or withdrawal from social interaction, gray or pale complexion, inability to walk a straight line, and shortness of breath at rest.*xlii*

Many hiking guides will recommend taking one's time climbing a high mountain. Some of these recommendations are to only ascend 2,000 to 3,000 feet per day above 8,000 feet. Staying with these guidelines, it would take about three days to make the Mt. Whitney hike. The level of oxygen at sea level is about 21%. At 12,000 feet, oxygen is reduced 40% per breath. Altitude sickness can occur at 8,000 feet but the more serious symptoms do not usually occur until over 12,000 feet. The rate of ascension is the main issue. There is no specific correlation to age, sex, or physical condition in who will be affected.*xliii* One can go well above these recommendations but he or she should understand the symptoms of dehydration and altitude sickness. The most effective relief is to descend immediately if the symptoms become acute.

In my training, I do not drink any water for my full time of exercising for two hours. This naturally, causes me to become dehydrated. I typically work out two-hours per day, five days per week and a shorter forty-five-minute workout by swimming, one day; and rest one day with only a 1.5 mile walk around the neighborhood.

My training method is to get my body used to a degree of dehydration. However, on the Mt. Whitney hikes, I begin drinking water early at breakfast and continue constantly until off the mountain. If one becomes thirsty, one is ALREADY dehydrated.

As a deterrent for altitude sickness, I take two aspirin as I begin the hike. When I reach Trail Crest, at 13,600 feet, I take another two aspirin. The aspirin cuts any pains I may be experiencing and I have been able to accomplish four out of four summits in the past four years. I have seen others who seem to hit a brick wall. They seem to begin to struggle for breath and have a very difficult time gathering energy to proceed up the mountain. One individual, who made the summit during my first hike, told me that he reached a point the previous year and just couldn't muster the energy to make another step, even though he could see the summit. Another individual, who accompanied me in 2011, told me that he would take a breath and two or three steps and have to rest. He DID eventually make it to the summit, but stated that it was one of the hardest things he had every accomplished.

In summary, you will need to train in sufficient time to get your appropriate muscles built and strengthened to handle the prolonged period of ascending and descending the mountain. You will also have to get your body acclimated to the altitude. Your body can do this but you must give it the opportunity. Training without hydration may help. A known deterrent for altitude sickness is to hike at or above 10,000 feet the day before your planned hike to allow your body about four to five hours of acclimation.

On the day of your hike, TAKE YOUR TIME! You are not in a race. A good slow hiking pace with frequent stops helps your body continue to acclimate to the altitude. Aspirin will help to relieve some aches and pains on the climb. If you are one that wants to race up the mountain, I suggest making the lower portion of the hike the slowest. That will give your body more time to acclimate. You can race from Trail Crest to the summit. At that point, your body will tell you whether it can run up the rest of the mountain or it will keep you at a slow pace due to your breathing. Finally, pay attention to your body. If it tells you through symptoms that it is just too high and needs you to descend, you may need to do so. Your life can be at risk if you should ignore its signals.

EQUIPMENT CHECK LIST

Documents

º **Permit** – you or the leader MUST have a permit to hike above Lone Pine Lake. Don't be invited to leave the mountain early because of this omission.

Route or Navigation Aids

º **GPS System**

º **Way Points** and Route Programmed into GPS

º **Compass**

º **Map**

Clothing

º **Shoes**

º **Extra Shoe Strings** or Laces

º **Extra Pair of Socks**

º **Cap or Hat** (ear protection would be great for cold, windy conditions)

º **Sweatshirt** (for mountain top, expect 30 – 40 degree F. temperature)

º **Waterproof Jacket** for 30 – 60 degrees F

º **Waterproof Pants** for 30 – 60 degrees F

º **Polyester Shirt** (will not hold water if sweating situation changes or cold-windy conditions)

○ **Cargo Shorts or Pants** (provides storage space outside backpack for easy access of items)

○ **Sailing Gloves** (provides warmth with finger-flexibility and protection for hands in a fall or spill)

Sun Protection

○ **Sunglasses** (especially necessary if a lot of snow exists on trail)

○ **Sun Block** (SPF 60+)

○ **Lip Balm** (SPF 15+ and non-scented, unless you want a hungry bear trailing you)

Hydration

○ **Hydration backpack** (2 –3 liters capacity)

○ **Water Bottle** (1 liter, extra water and aid in filtering and filling backpack)

○ **Water Filtration/Sanitization System**

Waste Management

○ **WAG BAG** – provided for each hiker by the Forest Service when getting permit

○ **Garbage Bag** – provides the opportunity to pick up wrappers and items others left behind

○ **Metamucil** or psylliam fiber supplement

Energy

○ **Food** – sandwiches, trail mix, nuts, jerky, whatever you determine to provide quick and sufficient energy, recommend 6 – 7,000 calories, minimum

○ **Extra Food** – plan on an emergency that you don't get off the mountain and must stay for an additional 12 hours or so

Night Vision

○ **Headlamp**

Protection

○ **Insect Repellant** – spray or cream, mosquitoes will be around from when you leave the Portal and welcome you at your return. Apply before starting out and again at the summit.

○ **Bear Spray** – If you are of small stature and hiking alone, you may want this. I have not found an issue with bears on Mt. Whitney. If you have a concern about bears or mountain lions, you can carry this in a holster until you get above the tree line. Bears appear to show very little activity above the tree line. Also, I have not heard of mountain lions on the mountain, but California has them.

Emergency

○ **First Aid Kit** – This kit should contain items to handle cuts and scrapes as well as blisters from chaffing.

○ **Emergency Blanket** or Space Blanket – One should definitely carry a "space" blanket for emergencies. This could be to keep warm because of a fall or just due to hypothermia. If one is incapacitated, warmth becomes a major issue. If you are not able to get off the mountain as planned, you should be prepared to survive a cold couple of nights. It may take 24 hours for anyone to realize that you are missing and may need help. You should plan on it taking 48 hours to find you.

○ **Whistle** – Just in case you fall off the path and/or need to get attention of a passerby, you need a whistle. This whistle should be on your person so that should you fall and be mostly incapacitated, you can reach and use the whistle. It takes very little energy to blow a whistle and the shrillness can be heard for miles.

Backup Items

○ **Batteries** – your headlamp, GPS, water purification device, and camera require batteries. Make sure you have backup batteries for EACH of these devices.

○ **Mirror** – Many compasses have a mirror incorporated in the assembly. A mirror may be quite helpful if you need to signal a helicopter or someone on another peak.

○ **Knife** – A multipurpose knife will be extremely helpful should you need to cut a bit of moleskin for a blister or to make a sling from your clothing to help with an injury.

○ **Small Scissors** – Scissors are very handy for shaping moleskin or duct tape to protect blisters.

○ **Flashlight** – a small flashlight to use, just in case your headlamp suddenly quit working.

Hiking Comfort and Safety

○ **Ice Axe** – An ice axe is very helpful if snow exists on the trail; a must in early morning travel over ice and snow. Learn how to self-arrest.

○ **Crampons** – Crampons are another great addition depending on the time of year or climbing conditions. If snow or ice is on the mountain, crampons can add safety in traversing through snow fields and may enable you to take a better path if the switchbacks are heavily snow-covered.

○ **Trekking Pole** – One or two poles help to relieve the back and legs from the strain of balance while hiking. It is also a major plus in going downhill to take the stress off one's knees.

Remembrance

○ **Camera** – A point-and-shoot digital camera will help to bring back and share your trip with your loved ones as well as remember this trek in later days and years. It is also an excellent way to record the magnificent starlit morning as well as the phenomenal sunrise.

○ **Award** – There are different Mt. Whitney medallions available on the Internet. These awards should be carried by the leader of all groups and presented to each one reaching the summit.

Hiking Breakfast

○ 3 **Eggs** wrapped inside paper bowl or_____

○ 2 or 3 **Links of Salty Sausage**, bacon or

_____

○ **Plastic Utensils, fork, spoon & knife** or

_____

○ 2 **Paper Plates and Napkins**

○ **Cooler** with ice, to carry breakfast items

CHECKLIST SPECIFICS

BACKPACK

Picking out the backpack you want to take on your hike up and down Mt. Whitney is like buying a car. There are many makes and models available. You will need to think about your needs and "must haves" to make this purchase. You may wish to think about how many hikes you will make AFTER Mt. Whitney. I planned on only making one trip but had such a great experience that I determined to do it again and again. After my next trip, I may decide to repeat the trip or hang up my backpack but I'll see how things go.

The major issues in purchasing your backpack are: weight, water capacity, loading flexibility, total storage capacity, ease of taking on and off, comfort, and ease of content access.

Weight

There will not be a huge difference in weight of backpacks but you are about to strap this contraption on your back for about eleven miles up a mountain and eleven miles back down. You, naturally, don't want to fall backwards if it is too loaded with goodies so pay attention to the weight of the backpack and its capacity. You will want it to perform well. Something that is light, insulated to keep your water cold yet keep your back warm in the early morning, flexible in handling your load of food, water, emergency items, sanitation items, extra clothing, etc.

Water Capacity

Water is going to be the heaviest load you will carry up and down the mountain. It weighs 2.20468 pounds per liter.[xliv] That means you will have over 6.6 pounds of water if you have a 3-liter backpack.

You will not find a water fountain above the Portal, where you start out. You will find streams and lakes up the mountain but the highest source of still water is a lake at Trail Camp or about 12,040 feet in elevation. The switchbacks offer water flowing down the trail but this source ends well before the 13,365 foot Trail Crest. The trail does offer a water source but I can't guarantee how many people have relieved themselves on the trail and their urine find its way into the water. You will be walking through this water source going up the switchbacks. I believe your best "last source" to be the lake at Trail Camp. It will be cold water but you will have to filter or sanitize it, as is the case with ANY water on the mountain. If you choose to refill your water supply at Trail Camp, you still have 4.3 miles and about 2,465 feet in elevation to climb to reach the summit. Of course, you have that same 4.3 miles to come back down without a source of water. It will take from three to six hours before you can resupply your water for the remainder of the descent.

On my trips, I take a three-liter water capacity backpack along with a one-liter sports bottle for extra capacity and also to use as a sanitization medium to gather water from the lake or stream and process the water. I typically drink about three liters of water reaching Trail Camp from the Portal. I like to stop at Trail Camp to rest and re-supply the water. On July 29, 2009, July 7, 2010, and on July 20, 2011, the lake was iced over with thin to thick ice layer. On July 18, 2012, the lake was cold but no ice. I believe this history would indicate that the water is going to be cold. In each case, I scooped out the water with the water bottle, and used my sanitizing pen (ultraviolet light) to treat the water and fill my backpack water bladder. After filling the backpack, I made one last scoop of water to fill the water bottle and treated it. This gave me four liters of water to make it to the summit and back. In the three previous hikes, I have used most of the water in my backpack and on my first hike in 2009, another hiker was out of water and I gave him some of the water from the water bottle. In 2012, I finished my 3 liters of water getting to the summit and drank the remaining liter on the way back to Trail Camp. Your water consumption may surprise you so take more than you think you will need.

A great benefit from the cold water from the lake is the way the water really quenches one's thirst. You may find the initial sip of water (water in the hose) has warmed slightly but after the first swallow of water, the following water should be extremely cold and satisfying.

The hydration backpacks are designed with a hose that requires a slight suction from the user and water is supplied right from the backpack. You will need to begin drinking water from the outset of the hike and as you gain in altitude; you will need to drink even more to avoid dehydration and altitude sickness.

In 2009, I hiked all the way from the summit to the Portal without refilling. I ran out of water just about 20 minutes from the Portal. In 2010, I stopped at Trail Camp to refill the water and rest. It made a TREMENDOUS difference in my attitude and awareness in the descent. Your goal should be to have water left in your backpack when you reach the Portal. Keep in mind that you MUST plan for emergencies. Water can make a huge difference in survival and comfort. Just as in the ascent, drink lots of water on the descent. You will be in the middle of the wilderness on the mountain. You should always make sure that you have plenty of water in reserve. Don't push your luck! If you had an accident going up, coming down, or falling off the main trail, do you have enough food and water to survive a couple of days? It may take a while to identify you as missing and get a search party to look for you. It is YOUR responsibility to be prepared.

Easy Off and Easy On

The backpack needs to fasten well to your body so it doesn't slide around or cause discomfort or chafing. You will need to feel comfortable that you will be able to put it on and take it off by yourself without anyone's help.

On my hikes, I take several breaks going up the mountain, trying to conserve energy and replenish the nourishment my body has consumed. When you take breaks, you may find yourself tending to keep the backpack on just to stay warm in the early morning. Eventually, on one of your initial breaks, you will want to take it off just to relieve the weight from your back and relax. Typically, a backpack has lower and upper buckles to hold it to your body and keep it from sliding around. When picking your backpack, think of putting it on and taking it off. Your fellow hikers will not be waiting in line to help you take it off or put it on. Everyone around you will be tired. You should feel it your own responsibility to take your backpack off and put it on. You need to also envision how the water feeding tube will stay out of your way in donning your pack and be in close proximity to place the tube in your mouth as you continue your hike.

Comfort

Some backpacks have webbed backing to ensure some airflow around your back while toting the pack. I thought this was very important. When it's cold in the morning, you will appreciate a close-fitting backpack to keep the heat to your body. The temperature when you start may be in the 40's and with your physical exertion; you will start to heat up. That is when you will need to have some webbing to allow the airflow to help keep your temperature regulated. When the sun begins to rise, you may notice you are warming up and even possibly sweating. You will appreciate airflow around your back at that point. Your first few miles to Trail Camp will probably get warmer and warmer as you hike. At Trail Camp you may begin to get some slight winds or begin to feel the cooling of the temperatures due to the altitude. I typically, find myself ready to don a hoody or extra clothing at that point. If Trail Camp feels warm, just wait about an hour when you reach Trail Crest. This is where the east/west winds meet and can really cool you down. Now you are back to wanting the backpack to stay on your back to keep your back warm. You may find that you really don't want to remove your backpack until you get to the summit and hide from the wind in the Smithsonian Hut. You mainly want to feel comfortable that your backpack will keep your back warm when you need it to and yet have sufficient airflow to keep you from over-heating at the lower altitudes.

Total Capacity

This backpack is your suitcase and/or briefcase for this hike. EVERYTHING has to go into it or your shorts' pockets. Just to review some of the items you will carry: compass, map, sunglasses, sunscreen, lip balm, extra shoe laces, food, water, extra socks, hat, pants, jacket, gloves, first-aid kit, aspirin, headlamp, fire starter, knife, water treatment system, Wag Bag, trekking pole(s), camera, insect repellant, space blanket, whistle, and maybe even bear spray.

It really sounds like a lot but it isn't too much. You won't need a 5 cubic foot backpack to take up the mountain because you need to remember that the more you pack into your backpack, the more the backpack weighs.

You will perform the act of a great grocery bagger. You are about to take a packing list and figure out where everything goes. You do NOT want to get a backpack just to hold the sufficient amount of water and nothing more. Poor planning may cause you to abandon your hike due to lack of energy and cold, because you didn't have sufficient food and clothing. Start with your packing list and determine what size you will need. I recommend several compartments in the backpack to allow you to put various items in locations for immediate access. When you want sunscreen or insect repellant, you want it. You won't want to have to totally unload your pack to find it.

Ease of Content Access

As I previously mentioned, when looking at backpacks, you will need to prioritize your emergency access items down to the nice-to-have-items. Your pack will probably have several compartments as well as little zippered access points. Take your list and determine what makes sense to you. I consider guiding equipment imperative as well as water and food. When I need to change my physical comfort for socks and extra clothing, I feel that I can "dig" for those items. I suggest planning according to your own personal concerns. Don't fret if you're concerned about some items like your camera's extra batteries. I recommend wearing cargo shorts or pants to provide extra load capacity to provide overflow capacity for your backpack.

External Loops

If the weather or condition indicates the need for an ice ax or crampons, you will want your backpack to have loops or some means of attaching your ice ax and crampons to the outside of your pack. You will want these items to be fastened securely so they don't hit you in the legs while hiking. Also remember that you have to pack out everything you took in. This means you will also have to consider where do you pack your Wag Bag if you had to use it? I don't believe you want to put it inside your backpack and thus need to determine where it might go on the pack.

Ice Water (side note)

You will really appreciate COLD water when you can get it on this hike. I recommend putting ice in your backpack water bladder the afternoon before your hike. Most of the ice will melt to deliver very cold water. When you prepare your breakfast in the last evening, fill your backpack with water from your room. You may still have some ice in the bladder from the previous filling. It will keep the water cold and give you a great cold-water source to start your hike.

WATER SANITIZATION DEVICE

Water on Mt. Whitney

You will see numerous streams and lakes on Mt. Whitney. The switchbacks have the last bit of water on the hike and you will be walking through this stream as it follows much of the path on the lower section of the switchbacks. The lakes are created from snow melt. The streams are created from the overflow of the lakes. The common element in this water is that animals including humans are not particularly careful where they use the bathroom and if the waste matter will flow into the stream or lake. ALL the water on Mt. Whitney should be considered a very probable source of Giardia lamblia. Even if the water source appears pristine, it can cause Giardia lamblia. The water MUST be treated. The following are various and easy ways to treat or disinfect the water for safe consumption:

Water Filter

Water filters are available in many styles and types. Most filters work by mechanically forcing water through a filter into a reservoir. These filters can be large and small, heavy and light. Should you decide to purchase a filter, check out the filter rate to determine how long it will take you to filter the water to fill the bladder in your backpack. You will probably need to plan on filtering two to four liters of water. Also keep in mind the weight and bulk of the filter. This will all add up in the end.

Purification Tablets

These tablets are typically iodine tablets that purify the water from bacteria. They are light to carry and easy to use. The drawbacks are the time it takes for them to act or purify the water and the taste it gives the water. Evaluate them as part of your sanitization processors. You may like them.

UV Sanitization Systems

There are very lightweight systems on the market that use ultra-violet light to sanitize the water. These systems are typically a pen device that is swirled in the water for about 90 seconds for a liter of water. A key to watch for in these systems is the battery life and type of batteries used. I used this type of system on my first three hikes and it worked great. I did find that my batteries weakened easily due to the cold temperature and I only received a few sanitization loads per set of batteries. Some of the batteries may be "photo" batteries which may make them more difficult to find in a rural setting such as Lone Pine. I have since purchased a new unit that uses common sized AA batteries but it does strongly recommend Lithium batteries and does NOT recommend alkaline batteries due to the shorter life span.

The mechanical water filter will be the heaviest and bulkiest of the three systems. However, it only requires mechanical energy to perform their magic. The iodine tablets will require the least space and weight but do have the drawback of taste added to the water and the time required to be able to begin drinking the water. Lastly, the ultra-violet pen is fast with no added taste to the water but does require batteries.

WAG BAG

The "WAG BAG" is a package that the U.S. Forest Service will provide for each member of the hiking party (included in the permit cost). They will give these to the leader of the group when checking in for the permits at the Visitor Center in Lone Pine.

The bag consists of a plastic sheet to be put on the ground. The hiker is to squat and defecate on the sheet. There is some toilet paper provided in the package as well as some powder to be used over the dung. The whole sheet should then be folded and sealed. The total package can then be hung on the back of the backpack.

Ron Upson with His Wag Bag

No, this doesn't sound too much fun to have to use one of these on the trail, but you will not have anywhere else to go, especially above Trail Camp. Your hike from the Portal to Trail Camp will have periods of trees and bushes where one can find SOME privacy just off the trail. After Trail Camp, the rest of the trail is quite exposed. Should one have to use the Wag Bag somewhere from Trail Camp to the summit and back, he or she may have quite a dilemma finding a spot with ANY privacy. This portion of the hike is on the edge of the mountain ridge where the path and rocks are totally exposed. You must bring EVERYTHING that you take into the forest OUT. This especially means human wastes! You can be fined should you choose not to obey the rules.

Your alternative choice is to get your body into a cyclic rhythm of going to the bathroom at the same time each day, preferably the first thing in the morning. This cycle would fit quite well with your hiking plans. I take Metamucil, and there are many similar fiber additives, before each meal. I find that I am almost as regular as an atomic clock. I still carry the Wag Bag, because there is always the unforeseen situation where I may need to go on the mountain. However, in four years, I have not even had the urge. I make sure that I am as "empty" as possible just before starting out, by visiting the outhouse located just a few feet away from the Portal. There is also a fountain for washing your hands just outside the building.

FOOTWARE

Soles

Your selection of hiking shoes is very important. Your feet are the basis supporting your whole weight and backpack going up AND down the mountain. Your backpack will probably weigh between 24 and 28 pounds. Then of course, consider that you have your clothes and normal body weight. Some people try to hike in tennis shoes but I feel the soles are just too soft to support your body when sticking your foot into or on a rocky crag or pointed rock. A typical "sneaker" would simply conform to the rock's shape and make your feet feel like they were in a vise or standing on a sharp point. The continued pressure on your feet could cause some very uncomfortable blisters to form and make your life miserable on the way back down the mountain.

I suggest looking for a hiking shoe or boot. The sole should have enough sole support to help you on those rocky points and not collapse if stuck into a rock crag. You may find yourself hiking about four miles on acclimation day, to and from Lone Pine Lake. This is where you will begin to really test your selection on the mountain, even if you've worn them many times before to break them in. On this preliminary acclimation hike, it is a mild walk with several hundred feet of "stair climbing", stream crossing on stones and wood timbers and the remainder is just a gentle incline and decline. The soles of your shoes do not need to be like steel and extremely rigid. You should be able to bend the sole but it should have quite a bit of resistance in doing so. When purchasing your shoes, you might try putting a chair on its side and step on the leg that is on the floor. It should give you an idea of how much support the shoes give over an irregular surface. If you like the feel, excellent! Buy them, but once you buy them, these will be your feet's best friends for about twenty-two miles.

Fitting on the Ankle

Another issue in buying your hiking shoes is to evaluate how high you like the shoe on your leg. Some boots will go over the ankle and others fit like low-top tennis shoes. Your hike on Mt. Whitney is an almost uninterrupted uphill eleven mile hike and the SAME coming downhill. Unlike many hikes on hilly or level ground, you will be hiking the same direction for maybe seven to eleven hours, one way. This means the amount of heel pressure you will feel on the downward hike will be constant. I hiked with boots slightly above the ankle for two years. Both years, I found the very back of my heel becoming chafed and irritated on the downhill portion of just the acclimation hike. That was only about two miles downhill. I had to use moleskin to support the skin around the chafing in both years. That did the trick but in 2011, I used a low-top boot with the fit like tennis shoes. I had no problem coming down from the acclimation hike or the hike down from the summit, the following day. When buying your shoes, see if you can find a slight downhill ramp in the store to get an idea of what the shoes will feel like on a downhill slope.

Size

Do you plan on wearing one or two pairs of socks? This is another question to ask when purchasing your shoes. I have always worn two pairs of socks when performing athletic activities such as football, basketball, tennis, etc. Naturally, I adopted the same strategy with hiking. When I purchased my shoes for the Mt. Whitney hike, I just bought my normal shoe size, for me, size 12. The shoes felt fine even with two pairs of socks. I used my shoes with two pairs of socks while breaking in my shoes and walked miles and miles with no ill effects. However, on my first two hikes, I found that my feet butted up against the front of the shoe and with two pairs of socks, it was quite crowded for my toes. The result was losing eight toenails after both hikes. It took a while for the nails to turn blue and finally come off. This was somewhere between a month and five months, before all injured nails came off and new ones finally began to grow. On my 2011 hike, using the low-cut shoes, I only wore one pair of socks. My feet were much more comfortable. I did end up losing two toenails but the loss was due to stumping my toe a couple of times on rocks. Some things just can't be avoided. I also did one other thing; remove my shoes for a few moments at the summit to change socks. My feet were really refreshed after doing this. I also removed them one more time at Trail Camp while I was refreshing my water supply and resting. Putting my feet up on a rock really felt good and gave me renewed energy for the remainder of the hike.

Extra Shoe Strings or Laces

You aren't through yet in the shoe store. Be sure to buy an extra pair of shoe strings or laces for your shoes. On my 2010 hike, I was wearing my shoes for the second consecutive year. I used the shoes on my acclimation hike and all seemed great for the main hike on the ensuing day. I arrived early to start my summit hike and as I got out of my car in the parking lot and put on my hiking shoes, one of the shoe laces broke. As I looked at them, they were both frayed and I had just overlooked it. I carefully, tied to broken string together and re-laced my shoes. I was very lucky that I was able to tie the string together sufficiently to make the hike. The realization came over me that I almost ruined my hike because of a simple shoe lace. I strongly recommend breaking in your shoes well before your Mt. Whitney hike. You will probably put some wear on your shoe laces during this period. You can just change your laces out before you hike but with such a little amount of weight and space for the extra laces, I just recommend taking them.

You should now have the information to purchase your new hiking shoes. You should also have sufficient time to break them in and make sure you are confident that you will like walking comfortably in them for about twenty-two miles, going up and down hill. You don't have to buy very expensive shoes; just get shoes that will give you support over the rocks, be comfortable on your heels and fit your feet without feeling crowded.

CAP OR HAT

You will need some type of head covering for your hike. It will be cool in the morning when you start out and when you get to the summit, you will probably find it cold and quite windy. You can lose a lot of body heat through an uncovered head.

Cap

If you decide that you want to wear a cap, see if you can find one with a neck cover. It will protect your face and neck from the sun. If you can't find a cap with a neck cover, you can use a bandana. Simply secure the bandana at the back of the headband of the cap and let it fall over your neck. You may also find that your cap is susceptible to blowing off once you get near the summit, particularly at the various windows crossings. You may have to take it off until you begin your descent.

Hat

If you decide to wear a hat, be sure it has a strap to either help secure it to your chin or hang around your neck to catch the hat should it blow off. A broad brim makes a great sail and you should count on it being windy at the summit.

CLOTHES

Polyester Shirt

I recommend wearing a polyester shirt versus a regular cotton shirt for your hike. Either shirt will work well at first. It will be cool in the morning when you start out and you should try to stay warm at the outset of the hike. Shortly, you will begin to sweat due to exertion. Cotton can become the enemy once your shirt gets wet due to perspiration. When you reach the Trail Camp elevation at 12,040, [xlv]you will find it rather cool and possibly cold. Polyester will not hold moisture, therefore once any perspiration trapped in the fabric evaporates, you will begin to warm. The cotton shirt would stay wet and make you feel cool in this high-altitude air.

Cargo Shorts or Pants

Cargo shorts or pants have extra pockets on them. Not only do they have the typical front two pockets and rear pockets, they typically have lower thigh pockets. You will be looking to keep some items in ready access should you need them. Here are some items you may wish to keep in your shorts or pants:

Permit – If you are questioned by a Forest Ranger for your permit, you will want to present it and continue on with your hike. Keep your permit with your shorts or pants.

Car Keys – You may have room in your backpack for your car keys but you certainly don't want to lose them. What if you took your backpack off for a few moments while you rested and a bear snuck up on you and stole your backpack with your food in it? Your keys would be going down the trail with the bear. Keep your car keys in a secure pocket.

Camera – You will need your camera in a place of easy access. Your photo opportunities are frequent on the mountain, so be prepared to quickly get your camera out of your pocket and start shooting photos.

GPS – If your GPS unit does not have a lanyard or arm strap to keep it around your neck or arm, you'll want to have it handy to pull out frequently to see where the next bend comes and listen to change in direction warnings.

Handkerchief – Your nose is going to run at times. You can carry tissue but remember you must carry everything out that you took in. This also means tissue. A handkerchief can at least provide a fast and easy way to blow your nose and wipe drips.

Lip Balm – Due to the dryness of the high-altitude air, you may find your lips will dry out quickly. Keeping your lip balm in your pocket provides ready access when needed and you WILL need it.

Sweatshirt

A sweatshirt or hoody can be a great asset as you climb higher on the mountain. I typically have been fine with my backpack over my polyester shirt to begin the hike. However, once reaching Trail Camp, I usually find myself getting rather cool due to the altitude and temperature. The lake at Trail Camp will still probably have a coating of ice on the surface. You will probably stop for a rest around this area and to also resupply your water. When the backpack comes off, you will find it gets rather chilly FAST. This is an excellent time to don extra clothing and the sweatshirt or hoody may be perfect. If you have a lightweight wind jacket that can handle cold temperatures, it may be even better. You will be climbing quite rapidly from this point and may begin to feel some wind starting to blow. The wind can cool you down very quickly. When you are descending, you may wish to take off your sweatshirt if you are warm. If you continue to wear it when you are warm, you'll find it can absorb the sweat and cause you to chill if you stop.

Waterproof Jacket

You can use the top of a rain suit if you have one. The main issue is to be able to totally block the wind or possibly rain or snow from reaching your body. The wind will begin around Trail Crest and depending on which way it is coming from, you will either have wind on the backside of the mountain or you will find it rather windy when you cross the "windows". These are short walkways between peaks that have no sides. It is like walking across a bridge between peaks.

In addition to blocking wind, the waterproof jacket will also protect you should you encounter rain or snow. At this high altitude, you certainly don't want to get wet. You are carrying everything you have on your back. Therefore, all clothing you carry will need to be light in weight and provide warmth.

Waterproof Pants

On my fourth hike, I finally donned my waterproof pants. I usually carried the pant bottoms of my rain suit. The pants can provide additional warmth if you are extremely cold at the higher altitude. You don't want hypothermia to set in so pay close attention to how warm you feel and your mental facilities. One of the first signs of hypothermia other than shivering is to begin to lose good common sense or thinking. In 2012, due to an early morning wind, I was much cooler than my previous hikes. The pants helped to shield the wind and keep my body heat confined. If you are cold and you don't feel something is right, just protect yourself and get more cover including putting on pants.

Sailing Gloves

Sailing gloves can be perfect on a hike because they do not have fingertips. The glove provides warmth for the hands yet without fingertips, they provide the nimbleness for your fingers to tie or untie knots without having to remove the gloves. I have yet to wear them, but other people hiking with me have commented on how much better they felt having worn them.

Prepare for ALL kinds of Weather

If the wind is blowing from the east or west, you feel a lot of wind until you get to the top of the switchbacks. If the wind is blowing from the north or south, you will feel the wind early, possibly in the first two hours of the hike. The wind will cool you down quite rapidly and the wind can blow from 10 to 50 miles per hour, depending on your elevation. However, if you experience wind early, don't give up on your hike until you see what it is like on the backside of the mountain. Many hikers give up too soon because they weren't prepared for the cold and the wind. Keep adding layers of clothes to make you comfortable. If you are cold, put more clothing on. If you're hot, take something off to be comfortable. If you haven't sufficiently planned, you can get quite miserable if you are cold and have nothing else to add. Your hiking will generate quite a bit of heat, but you will need to rest on occasion, and that is where you will start to really cool down.

SUN PROTECTION

You are hiking to an altitude of about 2.7 miles above sea level. At this elevation, you will receive mega-doses of sunrays. You will need to protect yourself.

Sunglasses

Polarized sunglasses can really help your eyes against the gray-shaded granite of Mt. Whitney. The granite can really reflect sunlight as you may first witness from the changing of gray rock mass in the early morning to a rather bright red mountain face at sunrise. If you are hiking in snow, be sure and put on your sunglasses to protect your eyes. The altitude may throw a headache your way just for hiking this high. You don't need to add insult to injury by having your eyes overly exposed to the sun.

Sun Block

There are many sun block creams, lotions, and sprays on the market. Your main focus is to get the maximum protection you can find. Sunscreen and sun block are listed in "SPF" or sun protection factor. The numbers indicate a percentage of blockages for UVB (Ultra-Violet B) rays. These rays are considered the rays that tan the skin. SPF 15 indicates screening out 93 percent of the UVB rays. SPF 50 would block 98 percent of the UVB. The key issue with the sun blocks and sunscreens are that they don't last very long. Using a high SPF will help to block a good portion of the sunrays you are encountering but in about two hours, your block is wearing quite thin. It needs to be re-applied. This would be another task to perform at the summit. One last recommendation on purchasing your sun block or sunscreen is to make sure it is "broad-spectrum". This means it not only blocks UVB but also

UVA rays. These rays are the little demons that cause your skin to age or at least show aging beyond its years.[xlvi] A simple selection of sunscreen or sun block is to get the highest SPF available. If you are looking for a tan, wait until you get back home and don't play with the sun power at high altitudes.

Lip Balm

You will find lip balm to be quite useful once you begin your hike. Your lips will start to lose moisture due to the high altitude. The addition of any wind will add to your lip's dehydration. Lip balm typically is sold in SPF ratings like sun block or sunscreen. Get at least SPF +15 and I also recommend non-scented.   Many brands have flavored balms. Just remember that you are in "bear country" at the lower section of Mt. Whiney. Bears have a terrific sense of smell. Bears DO love fruits and berries. So why attract a bear with fruity scent while you walk the trails?

INSECT REPELLANT

Insect repellant is available in several means such as lotion, spray, cream, etc. The main issue is to take some with you on your hike. A good time to put on your repellant is when applying your sun block just after breakfast.

When you begin your hike, you may sense some mosquitoes swarming when you are resting or going through some vegetation or streams. All this passes in a few hours so you will forget about the insect repellant until you get to the same point on the trail, coming back down the mountain. Your initial application of insect repellant should get you up the mountain without too many issues with insects.

As you come down from the summit, you will need to resupply your water. You probably have consumed from two to three liters of water from your ascent from Trail Camp. Since that time, you have not been near any water except on the switchbacks. As you come down the mountain, stop for a rest and to resupply your water, it is also an excellent time to reapply sun block and insect repellant. You will be about one to two hours before entering the "insect zone", around Trailside Meadows. At this point, you may notice some mosquitoes really hanging around. If you didn't reapply the repellant, you will feel them settle on your arms, neck, legs and places your skin is exposed. Just brushing them off won't necessarily make them leave. If you reapplied the repellant, you won't have to worry about this. You will still hear them around you but not be bothered by them actually attacking you. These mosquitoes can be unbelievably aggressive. Don't forget to reapply!

TREKKING POLE

Unless you typically do a lot of hiking, you may not have thought about getting a trekking pole. There is quite a variety of these poles on the market. They range from wooden sticks that are about forty inches in length to as much as sixty inches. Some people like to make their own and add character through rawhide string or carving designs and faces on the stick. Others on the market range from fixed sizes to adjustable lengths.

Do You Really Need One?

Like any issue at a party, there are as many viewpoints on the necessity of a trekking pole as there are ways to cook shrimp. The main point about a trekking pole is to add stability on the hike. There will be times you must cross a stream by stepping on stones. The trekking pole will help you balance to get across the stream without getting your feet wet. Just think of the discomfort of hiking some twenty miles in wet shoes and socks.

Two other factors that will favor a trekking pole; it relieves the stress on your legs on the uphill climb, and it helps you stay under control on your descent. On the climb, you will find some steps on the trail to be only two or four inches in height. Other steps can be as much as eighteen to twenty-some inches. You will be traveling with several pounds on your back and stability in climbing becomes quite welcome after a couple of hours. I feel the trekking pole gives me good balance in many situations and actually assists to lift me up high steps thereby allowing my arms to relieve some of the stress on my legs and back.

Descending down the mountain is probably the number one reason in my mind to take a pole with you. I felt a great relief in using the pole to help hold back my downward momentum. It isn't like you're going to run down the mountain, but you certainly get tempted to try. Remember, your descent will probably begin after seven to eleven hour of hiking uphill. Your feet will begin to put pressure on the front of your shoes. If your shoes are not fitting properly, you may begin to pack your socks into the toe section, putting pressure on your toes. The trekking pole can help you slow down and keep you under control. You can switch hands to help stay fresh.

I'm sure that you will probably read a couple of books on hiking Mt. Whitney (if you haven't thought of that you should just to get other opinions) and they will probably tell you that most accidents occur on the way down the mountain. You were very cautious and aware on the way up the mountain. You've taken some great photos of the night sky, the sunrise and panoramas at the summit. You've done it all and now you ONLY have to get back down the mountain. When you start tiring, you should definitely rest and get your strength back, but while you're trying to make your decision on when and where to stop, your trekking pole is an excellent ally to keep you under control and help to take the stress off the legs. They will be getting quite tired by now. Your arms haven't been taxed like your legs and can offer some great assistance.

What Kind of Trekking Pole Did I Get?

I visited my local sporting goods store and found quite an assortment of trekking poles. Some poles have compasses, some are rather ornate, some are adjustable and some are fixed lengths. I chose an inexpensive adjustable pole that would be easy to pack and if I grew tired of carrying it, one that I could easily put on my backpack. The adjustability was especially nice in selecting a comfortable height for the pole. For me, holding the pole at a very slightly elevated position from the bend of my arm parallel to the ground was perfect is gives me good support in lifting my body over high steps while giving me good support in the descent. When I finished, I am able to turn it into a two-foot stick to fit easily into my trunk.

In summary, a trekking pole serves the function to help one balance while crossing streams. It provides stability while walking. It provides an extra foothold in the snow when placed against one's shoe on the downward slope side. It helps to distribute the weight while hiking up the mountain and helps to provide a braking action to save the knees from downhill hiking stress.

WHISTLE

You should carry a simple whistle as a signaling device. Should you have an accident or come upon a situation where someone needs help, the whistle is an excellent way to get attention. It requires very little energy to blow and can be heard for miles.

Don't just have your whistle hidden in your backpack. It should be fastened to your backpack where you can easily reach it. If your whistle is on a lanyard, it will swing as you walk and get rather bothersome. Try to fasten it to a "D" ring on the front of your backpack with enough slack in the lanyard to reach your mouth but be fairly secure against swinging freely as you walk.

Remember, should you find yourself or others in unexpected difficulty, you will want to be able to reach your whistle and signal for help.

BACKUP ITEMS

Batteries

Change the batteries in every device that requires batteries the evening prior to your hike. You should then, have a FULL set of replacement batteries for EVERY device that requires batteries. Cold weather negatively affects batteries. You might have purchased batteries that have sat on a store shelf for a long time, so even your backup batteries may be old. Hopefully, the combination of "new" batteries to start the hike and a full set of backup batteries will handle your hiking needs. If you find that your batteries are losing power, you can eke out just a little more power by warming them up with body heat.

Mirror

Many compasses have a mirror on the back or some part of the compass assembly. This is a great backup system should you become disabled or come across someone who needs help. The mirror can be used to reflect sunlight toward hikers or helicopters should you need help.

Knife

A knife is an excellent tool. It can be used for cutting or prying things open. Should you need to cut shoestrings, clothing or vines, you will have a tool to help you get out of difficulty.

Small Flashlight

A small flashlight is an excellent backup. Should your headlamp batteries suddenly go out, it would provide some lighting to change the batteries, or a really bad case where the bulb went out in your and you didn't have an extra bulb, the LED flashlights give the brightest light and use little energy. You would still have a dependable light source. They will usually use either AA or AAA batteries that you hopefully have in backup.

FIRST-AID KIT

The first-aid kit is something that you will want to carry but hope you won't have to use. However, you may have a variety of reasons to use it.

Mt. Whitney is composed of granite, granite and granite, peppered with some vegetation like bushes and trees below around 12,000 feet. When you consider whether and why you need a first-aid kit, it is to help you to tend to minor cuts, scratches, blisters, aches and to prevent infection.

As you begin your 22-mile trek up and down Mt. Whitney, you should be rested and actually excited to get started. You will probably find yourself quite keen in the early portion of the hike. If you drink water constantly, stop frequently for short snacks and rest, and refresh your water supply so you never get low on water, you should find it an accident-free hike. But accidents do happen and usually because we push ourselves too hard. If you fail to take a rest stop when you need it, or slow down on the water intake or forget to have a little snack, your body may tire causing you to make some rather "dumb" mistakes. By being dumb, I simply mean that since you let yourself get a little excessively tired, you are greatly exposed to tripping, slipping or losing your balance. These situations can plant your face in the granite very quickly. On my first hike in 2009, I didn't stop for a rest once I left the summit. I became tired but didn't think much about it. I was just slightly below Trail Camp, simply following the trail and all of a sudden I didn't lift my foot sufficiently to cross over a stone in the path. My toe caught and I remember watching myself fall. I hit on both knees, elbows, and scraped my knuckles on both hands. I looked around because I thought it was a "Kodak moment" for someone if they saw it. I began to bleed at all the points mentioned. My trekking pole was now hard to hold due to the blood on my hands being slick. I wasn't too far from a stream so I just washed up a little and started out again. My knees continued to bleed for a while but my knuckles and arms just crusted over.

I must have looked quite a sight. Every now and then I would pass someone and they would kindly offer band aids or disinfectants, but I was still too much of a hurry to get down off the mountain. None of my wounds were bad enough to need stitches but it taught me a lesson. Lesson one, plan rests and make sure that they are taken. Lesson two, slow down and recognize when you are tired. You can avoid tripping if you just look where those opportunities exist. Lesson three; listen to others when they tell you that you are most likely to get hurt when you are tired! All the signs were there broadcasting to me to beware but I was too tired and too focused on finishing.

I packed all the items that I needed to tend to my injuries in my first-aid kit but didn't bother to pull it out. I am NOT recommending you do that. Fortunately, I did not have any infection set in and I healed adequately. You might as well use your first-aid kit if you need to. Your main issues will probably be similar to mine, where you have an accident and trip. Those opportunities are on and over the rocks, through the streams and even on a rather smooth pathway where you might just dig your foot into the path and trip. If you have an accident, take a few moments and clean the wound, disinfect it, and cover it to protect it.

I offer the following recommendation on making your own homemade first-aid kit:

o Tweezers

o Safety Pins

º Antibiotic Ointment

º Antiseptic Towelettes

º Wound Closure Strips

º Moleskin or Duct Tape for blisters

º Band-Aids, various sizes for various applications

º ACE Bandage

º Bandana (potentially for splints)

º Ibuprofen and/or Aspirin

º Antihistamine

º Gatorade powdered drink (for emergency electrolytes, energy)

Other items to accessorize your kit and have in the close proximity of your first-aid kit:

º Knife and/or scissors

º Signaling mirror to help get attention via sight. You should have a whistle already planned to be accessible at all times.

º Fire-starter (this would work at altitudes below 12,000 feet. There is NO wood above that to burn)

º Mylar (Space) Blanket. This can prove a life-saver if one becomes hypothermic and needs warmth.[xlvii]

You can find first-aid kits at your camping supplies stores. Check the list of included items or just assemble a kit yourself with the above items. If you find a good kit that you like but it is missing some items you want, just add them to the kit in your backpack.

I recommend storing the ibuprofen or aspirin in a ready-to-access area on your backpack. You may wish to take a couple of ibuprofen or aspirin as you start out on your hike and once again as you reach Trail Crest. Headaches are one of the altitude sickness symptoms. You may or may not experience this discomfort. I just try to avoid it right up front. After adding this to my regimen, I have not had any headaches on the hikes.

When packing your backpack, try to keep your first-aid kit in a good proximity for easy access. If you need the kit, you won't want to totally unpack your backpack to find it.

Your first-aid kit is there to deliver minor aid for scraps, cuts and chafes. If you do end up with a broken bone, you can use the bandana to aid in making a splint. In any case of a broken foot, ankle or leg, you will probably need evacuation off the mountain. There will be other hikers on the mountain when you go and I believe most would gladly assist you or your friends in getting you off the mountain should you need it. Otherwise, you may be asking someone to send help as soon as feasible.

COMPASS AND GLOBAL POSITIONING SYSTEM

Prior to my first hike on Mt. Whitney, I read two books, "One Best Hike Mt. Whitney," by Elizabeth Wenk and "Mount Whitney", by Paul Richins, Jr. Elizabeth Wenk indicated that since GPS worked on batteries, if the unit was dropped it may be incapacitated.[xlviii] Paul Richins, Jr. was more pro-GPS and pointed out that they work well in whiteout conditions where maps would be useless.[xlix] A global positioning system is highly technically oriented and does have weaknesses of battery life, banging against rocks such as dropping it or having it drop and submerge in a stream. A map and compass provides visual orientation for those who know how to use them. The maps are small and require calm, easy orientation in daylight to use. Nighttime use is difficult unless you know your star locations in the sky. For my hikes, I purchased maps of Mt. Whitney and a compass with a mirror backing. I also took a GPS with me.

After four hikes up and down Mt. Whitney, I strongly recommend a Global Positioning System. In my first trip, I followed a group from San Diego led by Chris Gonaver and his wife, Sue. They had a GPS and had little problem getting up and down the mountain. I didn't use my compass, map or GPS since I was trailing their group. On my second and third trip, being the only experienced hiker, I found two spots on the trail that were difficult to navigate due to the lengthy granite surface I was crossing over. I hiked this part of the trail in the very early morning, between two and four o'clock AM. Most of the trail is well identified with lines of stone or small stacks of stones to the path. However, you will see when crossing over such a large granite surface, there sometimes is no border to indicate the trail. Basically, the trail disappears. After "losing the trail due to the boulder surface", one would expect to see the trail to start up again. I found that I had to walk around the area at the end of the boulder surface to see if I could pick up the trail again.

On my 2010 hike, I walked around the boulder to eventually find a snow trail leading out. After a period of time, I found myself quite higher than hikers on a trail below. I should have backtracked to get to the lower trail but instead I tried glissading or riding the snow on my tail end. This is NOT a good idea for the weak at heart. I had planned on stopping at a rock surface below. Fortunately, I hit my target but had I missed I would have gone over a rock edge to some unkind rocks below. I gathered myself on the rock and found a path to get to the lower area where I had seen the hikers. Eventually, I found the hikers and their path through more snow. This was all I needed to get back on track. The difficulty with the glissading was I thought I could slow my speed with my trekking pole, but (early in the morning, it is ice and just looks like snow). The ice was so hard I couldn't penetrate it. I couldn't do anything about the speed of descent. My greatest luck was getting my slide to head toward the rock surface below. I almost stood up automatically with my speed and force by just putting my feet against the rock surface. I learned a valuable lesson to take an ice axe the next time.

On my 2011 hike, a friend, Pradeep Sharma, was leading across this same section of granite and we became disoriented and actually started back down the mountain. Fortunately, a couple of people were coming up the mountain. They asked if we had reached the summit and we said we were heading up the mountain. The group said they were doing the same. So I asked where they had just come from. When I was satisfied they had just come from the area we had previously hiked, I was ready to swallow my pride and head back up the mountain. Incidentally, they were following a GPS. I estimated our lost time was about 45 minutes.

In 2012, I programmed my GPS to guide me to the summit. I was excited to have it beep when I was near a turn in the path. It actually gave me a warning when my direction was about to change. Needless to say, I had much less anxiety and much more enjoyment in hiking in the dark during the early morning.

I am not in a race to beat my previous times up Mt. Whitney each year, but I do look for areas of improvement. The two aforementioned areas on the path where I experienced confusion was a concern for me. Eliminating the time spent hunting for the trail continuation reduced the confusion and therefore improve my ascent time. If you program your GPS with the trail and pay attention to it, it will indicate turns on your route and help to navigate through these confusing areas.

What is a Global Positioning System?

It is a device that uses satellites to determine the place on earth where one is located. It determines positioning in several formats. One format uses "UTM" coordinates, or Universal Transverse Mercator. Under this system, the world is divided into 60 north-south zones covering longitude six-degrees wide.l Two other systems use longitude and latitude by degrees, minutes and hours or degrees and decimally set minutes. Should you prefer a particular format an easy converter is available online at http://www.rcn.montana.edu/resources/tools/coordinates .aspx.li One simply has to enter the known formatted coordinates and look up the conversion to UTM, degree/minutes or degree decimal coordinates to use with your GPS.

Battery Life

On my first three hikes I have carried a GPS unit. However, I knew the unit only had an eight-hour battery life. Since these batteries were rechargeable, I conserved my battery life by turning off the GPS when not consulting it for a location. This meant that my GPS was not tracking my trail or path up and down the mountain.

After I identified the two spots on the trail that were consistently confusing me, I became very determined to find a way to avoid the confusion and be able to trek up and down the mountain. I needed to have a good hand-held GPS for hiking.

My first concern on a GPS unit was the battery life and how the unit's memory was affected by changing batteries. The one-day hike can take from nine hours to twenty-four hours. You will establish your own schedule. I am attempting to present the real experience that will help you plan your trip and provide the fewest surprises. Therefore, one of the first items to evaluate on the GPS unit you might entertain buying is how long the batteries will last.

After determining the battery life, the next question for your GPS unit is, "does replacing the batteries affect the GPS tracking system?" If the system resets itself once the batteries are replaced, nix that one and keep looking. You are NOT going to make this hike up and down the mountain in less than eight hours. You will need a long battery life and a unit that is not affected by changing the batteries.

If the system is not affected by changing batteries, this means the memory stays intact while the unit is without electricity from the batteries. In this situation, you can work with a battery life as short as eight hours. The main concern is to take a sufficient supply of batteries with you to make it through the total hike AND plan in extra time for unplanned events.

While one may think that the major issue on this hike is the first five or six hours because one is hiking in the dark, there is more to this. In all my three hikes, I did find that the same difficult spots still exist on the way down the mountain. This is in bright sunshine and in 2011; FOUR people were looking for the continuation of the trail on the way down. All of us had difficulty in finding the trail after we ran out of granite surface and looked for the trail to pick back up. We, all, walked around looking for the trail. Only after looking well out from the rocky surface did we see the trail pick back up. Using the GPS would have prevented all this confusion and saved time in hiking.

The available GPS units are very nice. One can pay plenty of money and get the same guidance of a lesser unit. Most GPS units will allow importing tracks to the device. This means the ability to download someone else's route from their GPS. Once downloaded into your GPS, you can simply see when you are going to make a left, right turn or keep straight ahead. Some of them will beep when approaching a turn.

I like backup systems to make sure that if one fails, I have an alternative. Therefore, here are two points to help you with your GPS. The first is the URL giving you a downloadable tract for the whole hike. It is http://www.travelbygps.com/premium/whitney/whitney. phd.[lii] This website also offers waypoints for various points on the trail. Simply download the route and track for your GPS to guide you on the mountain. Also, you should download the waypoints which will assist you in knowing specific points on the route. This track and waypoint information is formatted in Degree, Minute, and Decimal. Please remember that these waypoints are downloaded off the Internet and should be considered approximate.

WAYPOINTS OF MT. WHITNEY HIKE

Description	North	West	Elevation
Whitney Portal	N 36 35.290	W 118 14.426	8,360[liii]
Lone Pine Creek	N 36 35.220	W 118 14.707	8,609
Lone Pine Lake Junction	N 36 34.513	W 118 14.974	10,030
Meadow	N 36 34.300	W 118 15.383	10,331
Outpost Camp	N 36 34.263	W 118 15.509	10,384
Mirror Lake	N 36 34.249	W 118 15.725	10,633
Trailside Meadow	N 36 34.008	W 118 16.017	11,342
Trail Camp	N 36 33.847	W 118 16.682	12,014
Trail Crest	N 36 33.553	W 118 17.493	13,632
John Muir Junction	N 36 33.631	W 118 17.572[liv]	13,480[lv]
"End of Pinnacles"	N 36 34.344	W 118 17.437	13,410
Summit	N 36 34.717	W 118 17.519	14,505[lvi]

If you take my recommendation of an acclimation hike to Lone Pine Lake on the day prior to your main hiking date, you should be able to see how accurate these waypoints are on your system. You should be able to check Whitney Portal, Lone Pine Creek, and Lone Pine Lake Junction on that hike. It should either give you confidence for close proximity accuracy or cause you to use extreme caution on using these tables. As you might expect, one GPS to another could vary as much as 50 yards. Once you get an idea of a variance, you should be able to navigate the mountain.

Three areas to look out for on your ascent are the two granite surfaced areas, one above Mirror Lake and the other above Trailside Meadows. In these two areas, you will traverse over such large amounts of granite that you will not see a trail for many yards. Just be aware and keep looking for the trail continuation early and often. It should be dark when you go through these two areas, so it will not be easy. The more eyes you have looking for the trail, the less time wasted looking for it. The last confusion area is just past Trail Crest at the John Muir Trail (JMT) Junction. You will want to go to the right heading up the trail toward the Mt. Whitney summit. The trail to the left goes down the mountain and continues on the John Muir Trail.

Altimeter

Some GPS units offer altimeters. This can be an extremely cool feature when hiking Mt. Whitney due to its extreme altitude. You can almost figure out where you are on the trail by your elevation. It should help you calibrate your progress on the mountain.

Compass

If you are trying to evaluate whether to take a compass, I believe you should. The compass main enemy on accuracy is being right next to a big piece of metal such as a car. On the mountain, you won't find big chunks of metal to skew the compass and it doesn't require batteries. It does, however, require you to understand its principles and be able to read a map. Your GPS will provide more information in a matter of seconds, even including your direction. Should your GPS malfunction, your compass may provide information to make decisions on the mountain. If you are in difficulty during the dark hours, you may have to wait out the situation until dawn. Of course that comes fairly early due to your high elevation.

I recommend that all the parties hiking with you have a compass and GPS. Even though only one at a time may reference these items, if you happen to encounter situations where various people reach their limit on climbing and decide it is not good for them to reach the summit, those people would need to have a navigation system should they decide to start back down the mountain. Those continuing on would also need a navigational device.

ICE AXE AND CRAMPONS

An ice axe is long handled device with a sharp pointed handle and head looking like a pick. The head's end may have several designs to include a serrated edge to help hold onto a rocky or icy crevice. This design helps easily penetrate the snow or ice surface and use the axe as a short trekking pole.

I hiked Mt. Whitney twice without an ice axe and decided that I would rather have one with me. If your hike is before mid-July, you will most likely have snow and ice on at least four areas of the trail. It would stand to reason that August and September would have even less snow and ice but if storms have blown in during the summer, the high altitude can readily produce snow. This snow rapidly changes to ice as the snow melts during the day and re-freezes at night. The temperatures in the summer are typically in the teens and twenties on the summit in the early morning and twenties to forties at the Portal in the early morning.

The ice axe is usually designed with such a thin handle that it can be strung on the outside of your backpack. This means you can actually carry it up and back down without having to carry it in your hand. I found using the ice axe, as a second trekking pole was comfortable for me. I carried it on the mountain side of the trail. This allowed me to use it for stability to the mountainside of the trail while the trekking pole gave me balance and support on the downhill side of the trail.

The snow or what appears to be snow is hard-packed ice particles. In the early morning, it will be extremely hard to penetrate. On one of my acclimation hikes, the day prior to my main hike, I hiked to Lone Pine Lake and arrived about 9:00 AM. I tried to write my name in the snow with my finger and could only penetrate the icy snow about 3/8 inches.

On the Mt. Whitney hike the year prior, 2010, hiking alone, I tried to use my trekking pole to slow me down on the icy snow. I was at a higher location than I wanted and was trying to go to a lower trail. A snow field separated me from one boulder surface to another. I needed to slowly slide about fifty yards. I initially tried walking on the ice and rapidly determined that was not going to work. I sat on my butt and tried to use my trekking pole to slowly control my descent. This was a poor attempt at glissading. I couldn't penetrate the ice except for about ½ inch. I glissaded down to the next granite surface but luckily planned well on where I would run into the boulder. Otherwise, I could have gone over a short cliff for a distance. THAT is when I decided to keep an ice axe with me on my next hike.

Snowfield just below Trail Camp

In three prior years of hiking Mt. Whitney, I noticed three areas that have snow fields in July. Any earlier in the year would probably have even more snow. These areas are about 50 to 100 yards long. Other hikers have made a trail through the snow but the footing is icy in the morning and slushy in the afternoon. Either way it is slippery. You'll need to slow your pace to ensure good footing when in these areas. The ice axe handle provides sufficient length to dig into the snow or ice surface and provide stability. Two of the snow fields are just above Mirror Lake. The third is near the end of the pinnacles or just before you reach the Mt. Whitney summit. I really liked the stability on the slippery surface that the ice axe provided. From this experience, I plan on carrying an ice axe unless the Forest Rangers tell me there is virtually NO snow on the mountain. The weight of my ice axe is just about one pound. That may not sound like much but I want to be as light as possible. HOWEVER, the advantages of the ice axe on snow and ice far outweigh the effort of carrying the axe.

If you purchase an ice axe, be sure to either take some lessons on self-arresting or watch some videos on how to self-arrest. Self-arresting is a maneuver where you learn to fall using your ice axe to gain control of a slide and stop. This is extremely important should you be near some ice and snow on cliff-side trails. The ice axe also provides excellent speed control for glissading descents. A very good video is available to view online at http://www.5min.com/video/how-to-self-arrest-with-an-ice-axe-166577575.[lvii]

Crampons

Crampons are external ice shoes that clamp onto your shoe or boot. The crampon has sharp pointed spikes or blades that will provide ice cleats to travel on snow or ice.

I have not used crampons to date. I purchased a set for the 2012 hike and had them available if needed. After talking to the Forest Rangers when picking up my permit I was convinced there was so little snow, taking them with me was not practical. I believe the crampons would provide excellent stability in the snowfield portions of the hike. I do believe they could provide much easier hiking in the areas I previously mentioned. Crampons fit on the bottom of your shoe or boot and are held in place by straps. What you will have to weigh in taking them is whether to strap them on the outside of your backpack and stay away from the sharp blades or spikes, or to use carrying bags which allow you to carry them inside your pack.

If you hike Mt. Whitney in May or June or early July, you may need crampons to get by the switchbacks. This area can be closed in the earlier hiking season. Many hikers use their crampons and hike the chute with is just below the cables and basically straightens out the switchbacks into a straight uphill hike to Trail Crest. Again, other hikers will have blazed the snow trail for you to follow.

If you purchase crampons and take them, be sure to take them with you on your acclimation hike. There will probably be snow near or just above Lone Pine Lake where you can practice self arresting with your ice axe and using your crampons. As with the ice axe, you should also either take some classes on using crampons or at a bare minimum read up on how to use them. I found a good site at http://www.timeoutdoors.com/expert-advice/walking-advice/winter-talking/how-to-use-crampons.[lviii] It is your responsibility for your own safety and that includes learning how to use your hiking tools and make good decisions for yourself and your group.

MT. WHITNEY WEATHER FORECASTS

As Mt. Whitney hiking date approaches, it is an excellent idea to begin monitoring the weather. You will need to know the weather conditions and forecasts for possible road closures. Depending on how you travel to Lone Pine, if you are coming from the Bay Area of Northern California, you will have to cross the Sierras to the east side to reach Lone Pine. Check to see if the pass you intend to cross is open. Coming from Southern California or Nevada, you will not have that worry. You can travel on the eastern side of the Sierras without having to cross a high-elevation pass.

You can check current conditions online and get a seven-day forecast. The forecast will help you see if storms are predicted. If you begin tracking the weather a couple of weeks prior to your hike, you should have an idea of any accumulated snow on the mountain. The forecast will help you determine the temperatures at various levels that you should plan for. One good site I found was http://www.timberlinetrails.net/whitneyweather.html.[lix] This site provides current conditions and forecasts for Whitney Portal or the trailhead, Trail Camp or about half-way up the mountain and the Whitney summit.

COMMUNICATION

Using a cell phone in Lone Pine as well as on Mt. Whitney can be challenging. You may be able to find some spots where your signal is good and find other areas where there is no signal. Data coverage can be the same. I found about two to three spots on the Mt. Whitney trail where emails I tried to send but couldn't due to the lack of signals, would suddenly send or receive. You may even receive a phone call on the mountain but if you answer it, remember that you could lose your signal in the very next step you take.

Keep People in the Know

If you haven't figured this out yet, your Mt. Whitney hike can be quite enjoyable, however, it is filled with opportunities to get into REAL trouble! I am flabbergasted by the number of hikers that head out on the trail without telling their loved ones where and when they are hiking. Don't become a headline story in the news because you FORGOT to tell someone where and when you were going!

Permit Pick-up at the Visitor Center

If you are the leader or the solo hiker, you will have to pick up your permit at the Visitor Center in Lone Pine. Part of the process in getting your permit is to provide your vehicle license number, emergency phone number and names of the people accompanying you on the hike. Don't shortcut this process! The Forest Rangers want to know if a car is parked in the parking lot beyond the permit time, should they begin checking for that hiker's situation. You must provide all the information they request as a safety backup.

Immediate Family

Go over your plans with your immediate family. Tell them your intended path, when you intend to start and when you intend to finish. This also includes the acclimation hike. Anything can happen on the mountain. Make sure someone is aware that you are there and will receive confirmation that you have made it back to your intended spots.

Just to give you an example, there are two routes to start up the Mt. Whitney Trail. Many Forest Rangers take a short cut that is steeper but more direct in the ascent toward Lone Pine Lake. If you decide to try this path versus taking the normal Portal entrance and hike, make sure someone knows you are going on THAT path. I have yet to find a bear on Mt. Whitney; however, it is totally covered with signs that say "active bear area". John Linn, a friend of mine was on Mt. Whitney and took the shortcut. He encountered a bear just a little way into the hike. The bear charged him from a higher elevation but suddenly stopped and just wandered off. My point is that slight changes in plans can produce unexpected results. John wasn't looking for a bear but certainly had a great story to tell when he went back to the Portal.

Hiking Members

Make sure that all the members in your hiking group have the phone numbers of all the group families. If an emergency were to arise, you want to have all the phone numbers to make a timely communication to everyone. You don't want to have to start researching phone numbers once an emergency arises. You or others may be too frazzled to think straight.

All hiking members should also have the cell phone numbers of each hiker and his or her email addresses. The group may separate during the hike, due to some giving up and others just lagging behind. Make sure everyone knows to send a text message or email when he or she decides to turn back or reaches the finish at the Portal. You will appreciate knowing all your group has made it back safely without having to call each person and make sure he or she finished the hike.

Information to Communicate

Tell your family members when you plan to arrive in Lone Pine. Tell them when you expect to make your acclimation hike, what the intended hiking path is and when you intend to start. Give yourself and the group some leeway in the time and add some delays to prevent over-concern if you haven't checked back in with your family. Tell your family your planned return and a time that they should be worried if you haven't called.

For the hiking date, leave a copy of a Mt. Whitney map and your expected route with your family. They are available online so just print one off and explain your plan. Give them the expected time of your start and when you plan to finish. You will want to give them a time that they can begin to get nervous: give yourself some time for unexpected interruptions.

In 2009, I told my wife that I would be off the mountain by 7:00PM. I started receiving calls from my wife at 7:01 PM. Unfortunately for her, a very good friend of mine traveled from Mexico to greet me as I came down off the mountain. He humorously followed me down the mountain from the parking lot to the motel without my seeing him. As I rolled up in the parking lot of the motel, he pulled in right behind me. Surprised, I was talking to him while my wife was frantically calling on my cell phone. I should have added more time in the expected return. We

151

resolved the issue being "late" coming down the mountain and yes, I appreciated her concern. It's just SO easy to get sidetracked and be later in communicating than one expects.

Traveling Home

Just because you made it down from the mountain, don't leave your family in the dark on when to expect your return home. Lone Pine is about a three hour car ride to several main airports. If you are driving home that evening or the next day, remember that you have had a vigorous day hiking Mt. Whitney and your body will be TIRED. Let your family know your intended route home, when you might start your homeward travel and when to expect you. If you leave later than expected, be courteous and let them know you are heading out later than expected and readjust your expected return time. If you did become sleepy and have an accident, you want them to know your route so help can get to you. For you smart-phone advocates, there are apps that can track you as you drive, such as "Find Friends". There are other applications that will also show your family where you are on the road and how you are progressing.

FOOD AND NOURISHMENT

If you follow my recommendation of hiking one day to acclimate and the following day for your main Mt. Whitney hike, you will need to bring necessary food to cover the approximately 20 – 24 hours of hiking. The first acclimation day should be approximately five hours. Two hour up, two hours down and one hour at Lone Pine Lake. The following day would start with breakfast, food while climbing, lunch and food for the descent. Your hike may last anywhere from about eleven hours to as much as 22 hours. Your stamina, group size, and lengths of rest will specifically determine the length of the hike.

I recommend taking a food that is easily carried in your backpack, that won't melt, won't spoil and food that you LIKE. You should also carry a different food as a reward for your two lunches, acclimation and Whitney hikes. Again, lunch should consist of something that can handle traveling in your backpack with everything else you will take and can handle the weather elements of heat, cold and no refrigeration.

If you are worried about calories, this is one time you can probably get away from that worry. I estimate you will probably use from 6,000 calories for your main hike to as many as 9,000 – 10,000 calories. If you want a simple way to estimate your calorie usage, try this on a treadmill. Many treadmills ask for age and weight of the user. Select about a 15-degree rise for one hour at about 1.5 – 1.8 MPH. Walk on the treadmill for about 10 minutes to get the estimated calories used. This should be about 1/6 of an hour's calorie consumption. Multiply your calorie usage by 6 to determine your hourly hiking calorie rate.

Remember that you also have a backpack with water, food, and accessories that will weigh between 24 – 28 pounds. Reset your treadmill to your age and now add about 25 pounds to your weight. This would be an approximate weight for your backpack. That means you are reentering your age, your weight plus 25 pounds (for the backpack), setting the incline for 15-degrees and speed of 1.5 – 1.8 MPH as done previously. Note your calorie usage at the end of ten minutes. Multiply that number by 6 since the 10 minutes is 1/6 of an hour. Your total is approximate hourly-calorie consumption. You can now estimate how many calories it takes to carry your full weight, including your backpack per hour on Mt. Whitney. If you wish to see just how many calories are burned by carrying your backpack, subtract your previous 60-minute figure without your backpack from the one including your backpack. In my case, I will use approximately 100 calories per hour just to carry my backpack. This is not a very scientific means of determining your calorie usage but it is simple and NOT that far off. You want to have a great experience on this hike. Don't underestimate how much food you will need to keep your body energized. If you don't feed your body, it will become fatigued and that is when accidents really start to happen and the body starts to fight you back with cramps.

Hiking Foods

Now that you have an idea that you can really burn up some calories, it should make sense that you can take some energy foods that you may not normally munch on. I make the following six hiking food suggestions:

1. Trail Mix.

There are many trail mix varieties available from grocery stores, membership stores and a wide variety of organic and health food stores. The general make up of trail mix is nuts, raisins, pretzels, and candy-covered chocolate. If you want to add a little more salt to your intake because of the sweating that you may experience below 12,000 feet, simply add salted peanuts or almonds. In all, this mix will provide great energy from frequent rest breaks of about every two hours.

2. Beef or Turkey Jerky.

This is a favorite of many hikers due to the high protein, fat and salt delivered in each strip. There are a great variety of flavors and you should be able to find something that fits your bill. I personally like to use jerky as my lunch. I like the flavor and it is a great reward for lunch and for reaching the summit.

3. Sandwiches.

Sandwiches are a general crowd pleaser. Leave out the watery elements such as tomatoes and cucumbers. You will be looking for flavor and protein. If you can get flat bread or harder bread that won't squish if it is stuffed in your backpack, you may prefer that.

4. Camping and backpacking food.

These are prepackaged meals prepared to simply tear open the package and consume. These foods are at your outdoor stores that cater to hiking, fishing, hunting and camping.

5. Energy bars.

Many outdoor retailers as well as health food stores offer an array of energy bars. These bars are full of nutrients to provide energy in a small package. They are very good to resupply one's energy almost immediately.

6. Chocolate

Chocolate has sugar to quickly fight fatigue, caffeine to pick you right up and fat to provide fuel for hiking. Just keep in mind that it may melt and become soft and messy. You might need to lots of water to wash your hands after it melts which is very scarce on parts of the mountain.[ix]

As you look at the foods you need to take with you, keep in mind that everything that goes with you up the mountain must come back off the mountain WITH you. Food packaging will have to be stuffed back into your backpack to take with you on the remainder of your hike. If you look at items that can be repackaged into plastic bags, it is easy to stuff opened bags into other bags to conserve space. I personally like repackaging trail mix into smaller bags of about "10-minute" consumable sizes. This is a good amount to enjoy on a break and the bag is easily stuffed back into my backpack. As I said, I like jerky for my lunch and it is usually packaged in small bags for an almost perfectly sized lunch.

Plan for using a bunch of calories and need to replace the energy used while burning calories on your hike. Don't forget that you will also be hiking in the wild. Even though there are Forest Rangers in the area and other hikers, if you have an accident that takes you off the normal trail and you are immobilized, you may have to spend longer than anticipated on the mountain. You should take this into account when planning your food supply. Take MORE than you will need JUST IN CASE! It is much easier to put your excess back into a jar, cooler or bag when your hike is over than to almost starve because of an unexpected event.

HEADLAMP

Night vision with a headlamp

When you start hiking Mt. Whitney before mid-night or in the early morning on your hike, you will spend more than 4 ½ to 6 hours in darkness, your headlamp will be one of your BEST friends. A flashlight just won't cut it since it requires holding it and pointing it in the direction you want to see. Headlamps fit on your head or over your cap or hat and illuminate the ground in front of you wherever you look. Here are some suggestions on what to look for when shopping for your headlamp.

Beam Distance

The brightness is not as important as the distance the light will illuminate. You will need from 20 – 30 feet of illumination to give you plenty of forewarning of difficulties on the trail. You won't have to illuminate the whole trail. You will just want to be able to see ahead and get a good idea of what you are about to encounter.

Bulb Life

You will find more uses for the headlamp than just making your Whitney hike. It is very useful for many other activities like running for exercise before sunrise. If you need to work in dim-lit areas around your house for projects, the headlamp is always looking at the same thing you are. You'll find it helpful to use when working under your sink or under your house. Therefore, keep an eye on the expected bulb life. It may be the deciding issue on when you will replace your headlamp.

Multiple Bulbs

It really doesn't matter how many bulbs your light has as long as it will deliver the illumination distance you need and use as little battery power as possible. I always recommend having extra batteries but common sense tells you that the more bulbs the shorter the battery life.

Lux versus Lumens

Lumens indicate a rough approximation of the maximum light output. Lux measurements at a specific distance are a more reliable measurement for choosing headlamps.

Battery Life

No matter what features the headlamp has, pay close attention to the type of batteries and the battery life. Many headlamps use AAA batteries that are small, light and easily attainable. Beware of more elaborate battery sizes or types. You can use rechargeable batteries but make sure they will last for a longer period than you anticipate being in the dark on Mt. Whitney. Six- to eight-hour battery life should be more than necessary for your need. Some headlamps will blink when the battery life is about to give out. This is an excellent feature to warn you to stop, take out your extra batteries and change them.

Filters

Many headlamps come with a variety of colored filters. In hiking Mt. Whitney, you will be mainly interested in the regular white light or un-filtered. However, remember that this is a light source you can use at home and in other situations. I like astronomy and the red filter is excellent in preserving night vision. There are also, green, and blue filters available. Consider what other uses you may have for your headlamp and buy accordingly.

Waterproof

Waterproof and water-resistant are two very different terms. Waterproof will usually give you a depth the lamp will withstand when immersed up to a specific time. Water-resistant means the light will withstand rain but if it falls into a stream, it may go out immediately, not surviving the ordeal. Water-resistant is probably all you will need. If you plan to use the headlamp outside your hiking activity in a more water-bound environment, you may wish to look for waterproof.

Lithium-ion versus alkaline batteries

Lithium-ion batteries are lighter, perform better in cold weather and hold a charge up to ten years. However, alkaline batteries are more readily accessible on the market worldwide. You may have to evaluate your headlamp usage. The alkaline are less expensive.[lxi]

Remember when you are hiking that while your headlamp is on, if you look at your hiking partner(s), your light is shining directly in their eyes. You will discover the same happens in reverse. When you take a rest break, either turn off your lamps for a few moments while you talk or just don't look directly into someone's face.

CAMERA

Hiking Mt. Whitney during the early morning hours has two fantastic advantages. You can take some night photographs on the trail and you can also get some fantastic sunrise photos. Most of us are used to light polluted skies which mean too many people have no idea of what the Milky Way looks like except in a photograph. Lone Pine and Mt. Whitney do not have light polluted skies. In the high desert like Lone Pine and especially on Mt. Whitney, you will see stars that you may not be able to identify even in constellations you know because they are camouflaged with so many other stars. Some people wonder why the clouds in the sky take so long to move across the sky, only to realize they are looking at the Milky Way. There are SOOOO many stars that they appear to be a cloud. You have an opportunity to not only memorialize your trip but to add some unimaginable photographs along the way.

Night Time Sky Photos

Night time sky photos are photographs recording the stars in the sky or a combination of terrestrial artifacts with the night sky. You will need a camera and probably the owner's manual to help you determine some features you may or may not have ever used before. I will list features that can make your photos better but if your camera is lacking in some of these areas, don't fret! Just try to understand the principle of the photography and work with what you have.

Camera

You will need a camera that has a manual exposure mode, meaning you can select the length of the exposure.

You will also need to have a photo delay feature in taking pictures (usually 2 seconds to 10 seconds), or remote control shutter release to minimize the shaking when taking pictures. Just the pressure of pushing the button to take a picture will cause the camera to jar and this shaking will show in your photo. You will need to be able to select your ISO setting. ISO means International Organization of Standardization.[lxii]You will need to have a RAW setting on your camera which means your camera will not compress the information and give you full latitude in processing the results.

Small Tripod

Your second almost "requirement" is a small portable tripod for your camera. This type of tripod is about six to seven inches long, light and easy to pack in your backpack. Unlike daylight photos, night photos are extremely sensitive to vibration and taking pictures of the sky will require an absolutely steady camera. Just your breathing while holding the camera will cause movement in the photo. You CAN lay your camera on a rock but it is hard to direct the camera in the skyward direction to get some trees, rocks or other foreground objects included with the stars or moon in the sky. The camera just screws onto the tripod and place it on a rock hard surface to position your camera in the direction for the photo.

Setting up your camera

Turn your "auto focus" off. You will want to set your camera to "infinity" focus. Set your ISO as high as you can get it. This allows as much light as possible into your photo and reduces graininess. Set your exposure to 30 seconds. If this is too high because of the amount of light from your ISO setting, you can and will probably adjust your exposure down in time. Set your f/stop to as low as you can get it. Finally, set your timer delay from 2 to 10 seconds.

Take Sample Shots

Your eyes cannot see as good as your camera. If you take some sample shots around the area, you can get an idea of what good photo subjects exist in that spot. It also gives you the opportunity to decide if your camera is setting properly on your tripod and make appropriate adjustments to center and achieve the photos you want.

Preventing Star Trails

There is a "rule of 600" to assist you in preventing the stars in your photo from elongating or showing the effects of the turning of the earth. Find your owner's manual to see the focal length of your camera lens. Simply divide 600 by your focal length to get the maximum time of exposure without showing star trails. For example, if your lens is 21 mm, 600/21 = 28 seconds would be the maximum exposure to avoid star trailing.[lxiii]

Practice

You need to practice this process before your Mt. Whitney hike. If you have a chance at home before leaving for the hike, practice a few times to get familiar with your camera and how to set it up and shoot some photos. Another good time to practice is the first night you arrive in Lone Pine or surrounding area for the hike. Even if you have car lights going through the picture because you may be shooting across the highway toward a mountain, the results can be quite interesting. That is the whole point of night sky photography, to get foreground images combined with the sky.

Possible Targets

Some good targets in your backyard or in the motel parking lot are to include some trees with the sky. You will also find that the slightest amount of light brightens the foreground and coupled with the stars shining in your picture, provide an image that you may never have seen before. Should you wish to highlight some of your hiking partners in the photo, simply either use a flash or use your headlamp to "paint" them into the photo. Where ever light hits, the object will look almost like a day photograph, yet the stars in the sky will also shine in your picture, to give you an awesome picture.

Taking pictures on the Trail

As you begin your hike, it will probably be very dark. After you have hiked about an hour, it is a good time to take a short break and just take a few pictures. Fasten your camera to your tripod and set it on some rocks on the side of the trail. Take a few photos of the surrounding areas and of the sky. It is also a good time to take some regular photos using your flash to show what is all around you at this point on the trail. Finish by having a snack to eat and get started back on your hike. You may wish to extend just a little time of each rest to include some photos.

Sunrise

Sunrise from just below Trail Camp

The sunrise on Mt. Whitney is one of the most picturesque you may ever see. The dawn will begin with a light blue showing in the east. You will eventually see some red begin to appear. No matter where you are on the trail, this is the time to stop and start taking sunrise photos. The sky will begin to get redder and redder with each passing second. Eventually, you will see some peering of the sun on the horizon. Keep shooting! As the sun continues to rise, it will change the sky colors. You can always delete a poor photograph or shot you don't like, but you can't create one if you stop and miss the "perfect sunrise".

Mountains turn red at sunrise

Now is the time to turn the other direction and look at the mountains toward the Whitney summit. These mountains will begin to turn a beautiful red. Keep shooting to get the varying degrees of red. You can cull the pictures you don't like later. After the mountains begin to lose its redness, you can continue on your hike. Just don't miss this opportunity. If you have clouds in the sky, they will help to produce an even MORE magnificent view. In my four years of hiking Mt. Whitney, I have yet to see a sunrise I would call ordinary or unspectacular.

If you like taking night sky photographs, you can read up on more techniques online. You may wish to also learn how to stack photographs. This is a process that takes each photo, aligns them and intensifies the light exposed in your photograph to produce more striking results. This is how astro-photographers are able to get pictures of nebulae and galaxies from such very little light.

BACKTRACK STRATEGY

When one hikes in a strange and unfamiliar area, he or she should always be prepared to go back the way he or she came. As you start your hike, occasionally look back to see the trail from a new perspective. You will have developed a sense trail familiarity should you have the necessity to return over your traveled path.

You may find times that you either don't see a continued path or realize that your current path is beyond your capabilities or comfort level. This is a time to stop and assess the situation. Is there a safer way or are you off the trail? If you determine that there is a safer way, make sure that the trail docs continue after you get by this area of concern. If you have doubts that you on the trail, it is a good time to turn around and retrace your path until you get to a point you are confident about the trail. Having doubts of your location on the trail is common. Your GPS may tell you to take a specific turn and you find out that the turn should have been back or forward another 20 or 30 yards. Returning back on your path until you reach familiar territory will help you make better and safer decisions on your hike.

COMMON SENSE

Common sense is defined as, "sound practical judgment that is independent of specialized knowledge, training, or the like; normal native intelligence."[lxiv]

Hiking Mt. Whitney is inundated with question marks as to your own common sense. I have seen people sitting on a rock about three feet in diameter and about 1,000 feet or better above the rocky floor below. These people had climbed up to this peak and seemed to enjoy sitting there in an area you certainly couldn't put ME. I am somewhat afraid of heights and this perch would not be on my top-ten list of things to accomplish.

On Mt. Whitney, you will be constantly challenged with "common sense" decisions. They may be as simple as "how do I cross this stream?" It may be that you are in a snowfield and need to get to a lower elevation. Do you glissade down? Once one starts to slide on this icy surface with gravity involved, he/she has hopefully, calculated the sliding path and where he/she will end up. On Mt. Whitney, one can easily slide right off a cliff.

A simple task like communicating with your family to let them know when and how you intend to make your hike is good common sense. Take a few moments and "Google" the movie, "127 Hours." You will see what happens when a person doesn't communicate the hiking plan.

My main request is that you think through all the issues you can and try to prevent problems that might arise. Many of those situations are just COMMON SENSE. Don't leave your common sense at home!

AWARD

Presenting each one in your group with an award for reaching the summit has a magical effect on an individual. Reaching the summit is quite a feat. Each person will hopefully sign in the visitor log and take pictures on the summit. In 2012, I took a small medallion for each hiker to the summit and presented those who reached the summit with their award. Their faces told the story. This little piece of metal was given to them at the highest location in the contiguous U.S. It is a treasure I believe they will keep and cherish.

I found medallions available on the Internet. One medallion is rather large but it does have room to engrave the hiking date on the coin. The other medallion is under $10.00 in cost and still provides a treasure to commemorate the accomplishment. I suggest doing your Internet search for "Mt. Whitney medallions". Several sites came up with that query. Two of the sites are: https://store.nwtmint.com/product.../Mt. Whitney Bench Mark/ for the engravable coin and https://store.nwtmint.com/Mountaineering/Mt. Whitney/ for the smaller medallion.

Sam Moore with His Award

PRECAUTIONS – WHAT TO LOOK OUT FOR

THUNDERSTORMS

When one hikes Mt. Whitney, he or she needs to start checking the weather reports for Mt. Whitney about ten days prior to the hike. This is the highest mountain in the contiguous United States, at 14,505 feet. During the summer months, warm air is blown from the central valley where plenty of moisture is evaporated from the agricultural area in the valley and this moisture is compressed as it rises about 14,000 feet to the peaks of the Sierras. With such high altitudes and accompanying cold air, the air can easily become quite unstable when mixed with the warm, moist air producing sudden thunderstorms.

Depending on the time of year you are hiking Mt. Whitney, the weather report may call for possible afternoon thunderstorms in the Sierras. If you see this forecast, definitely plan on hiking early in the morning and reach the summit before 11:30 AM. There is no guarantee that summiting by this time will avoid the thunderstorms but most information you will find regarding thunderstorms on Mt. Whitney indicates this weather normally occurs after noon.

On July 29, 2009, I hiked Mt. Whitney and reached the summit at about 11:00 AM. I could see dark clouds accumulating in the southwest. I felt that I needed to get off the summit fairly quickly. I spent about thirty minutes on the summit and began my descent at about 11:30 AM. When I reached Trail Crest, it began to snow. It wasn't a thunderstorm but to me at the time, I certainly thought it could be and the weather pattern of afternoon showers even though it was snow, held true.

Sign in the Smithsonian Hut Regarding Lightning

There are a few considerations in regard to thunderstorms on Mt. Whitney. One element is that you are TOTALLY exposed on the summit. There is absolutely NO shelter from lightning. One could hide under some rocks or talus but when wet, they can carry electricity quite well. There is also the Smithsonian Hut on the summit. It has a metal roof and is built of stone. There have been several deaths over the years where people took refuge in the hut from thunderstorms. Don't play with nature on top of Mt. Whitney! She usually wins! Get off the summit as soon as threatening weather begins to show. Once you are off the western face of the mountain ridge, or back to Trail Crest (about a two hour hike); you may feel a little safer from the lightning. But you are still exposed to the elements all the way down to Trail Camp, another 1 1/2-to 2- hour hike.

If you were playing golf on a golf course and you found yourself in violent lightning, I doubt you would continue to play. You would probably head into the clubhouse. I don't think you would head for a tree (a definite lightning rod just like staying on the summit), or stay in the open ground on the fairway which is similar to staying at the higher altitudes on the rocky surface of the Mt. Whitney Trail. Your best bet is to get a forecast, plan your hike with the possibility of a thunderstorm. You will mainly need to reach the summit in the morning, give yourself time to enjoy it and get off the mountain top before problems can arise.

I am amazed by the number of people who start out late and plan on reaching the summit in the mid to late afternoon. In 2009, I passed many hikers, maybe thirty to forty, hiking to the summit when I was heading down. Had the weather produced thunderstorms, they would have been in deep trouble. You are in charge of your OWN safety. No one will act as the parent to make you leave the summit. Just get your butt off the summit if the weather starts to look threatening!

HYPOTHERMIA

Hypothermia is the condition where the core body temperature falls below the required for normal metabolism and body functions.[lxv] When you begin packing for your trip to Lone Pine and the ensuing hike on Mt. Whitney, you will be caught in a dilemma. If you pack all the clothes you think you will need, you would almost need a suitcase to take up the mountain with you. If you ignore your intuition, you could become quite uncomfortable during your hike.

When you start out, the temperature at the Whitney Portal will be probably somewhere 30 to 40 degrees F. Always check the current temperatures and forecasts online before leaving for Lone Pine and get the most current information the day prior to your hike. As you start out on your hike, you may be quite warm with your backpack insulating you from the outside temperature and reflecting the generated body heat back toward your torso. Even on your rest stops, you may find yourself quite warm and enjoy taking off your backpack to cool off. At the early stages, you should wear a polyester or non-cotton/non-wool shirt or top that captures sweat and can really cool you down. When you reach cooler temperatures higher up, you will be glad your shirt or top doesn't keep the moisture sweated out earlier in the morning.

When you reach Trail Camp, you will be about 12,040 feet in elevation. You will probably see the lake covered in ice. You may want to add a layer of clothing at this point while you filter or sanitize your water and refill your supply. If you're not too cool yet, don't worry, as you get to the Trail Crest, you will begin to feel the winds that are probably coming from the west or east. It just gets windier at Trail Crest. If you are cool, go ahead and put on a sweater or hoody. It is going to get colder and windier when you reach the summit.

In the next two to three hours, you will hike by the "windows" that may have some very spectacular wind gusts to remind you that you are high up and are about to reach an area that is quite cool. Just be aware of how you feel and make sure if you are getting cold, put on extra, warm clothing to warm back up.

When you reach the summit, you will probably find it windy. You may even find it WINDY! During my first hike on July 29, 2009, it was a little windy but not too cold. I put on a rain slicker to cut the wind and was fine with the temperature. On my July 7, 2010 hike, I was extremely cold, even with the same rain slicker I wore the year before. The temperature felt like it was about 35 degrees F and the wind blowing about 40 to 45 miles per hour. I could barely stand against the wind. I spent one hour on the summit and had to start back down. I was REALLY getting cold.

On July 20, 2011, on my hike to the summit, I donned a hoody along with my rain slicker at Trail Camp. When I reached the summit, I was so cold that I signed in on the log at the Smithsonian Hut and just went into the hut to get out of the wind and cold. I stayed there most of the time, about one hour, on the summit and then headed down. Again, it was about 35 degrees F. but lesser winds of about 30 miles per hour.

In the three of the four summits I have made on Mt. Whitney, it typically was cold and windy. This combination is a perfect storm for hypothermia.

Only you know how you react to cold temperatures and wind. If you feel that you will be challenged to stay warm, you can pack a jacket on the outside of your backpack. Just plan to have enough protective clothing to keep you warm. One backup plan listed with the equipment list is a space blanket. This is a very lightweight blanket that reflects heat. If you become too cold, don't hesitate to un-pack your blanket and warm up. You can hike while wearing the blanket or take a little time to just rest and warm up. Remember, you are responsible for your OWN health and safety.

Hypothermia starts with shivering. The muscle action provides warmth to the body even though you might not think you are warming. When the body begins to shiver more violently, it is a sign that things are getting serious. One begins to lose coordination and may experience mild confusion. As one's temperature continues to drop, one may have difficulty speaking and have difficulty in using one's hands and possibly even beginning to stumble when walking. As you can imagine, trying to hike back down a mountain of rocks, next to cliffs on both sides, is not a place to start experiencing hypothermia. If you need to "pull over" on the trail and warm up, do so! You need ALL your facilities to make this hike[lxvi].

The main areas of concern, in my opinion, are from Trail Crest going up to the summit and back down to Trail Crest. This is about a five- to six-hour period of hiking and spending time on the summit. When you are walking, you will usually feel fine because of the heat produced from hiking. However, if you get cold, you have to get your body temperature back up to standard level to feel normal again. Otherwise, you will find yourself shivering and being quite uncomfortable. One side note is to keep an eye on your hiking buddies. They may shrug off the signs of hypothermia until things get serious. If someone complains of being cold or shivering, just keep an eye on them.

ALTITUDE SICKNESS

Altitude sickness is one illness that ANYONE setting foot on Mt. Whitney is susceptible. It is simply symptoms emitted by the body due to lack of oxygen. Acute Mountain Sickness (AMS) is caused by four factors, high altitude, fast rate of ascent, high degree of exertion, and dehydration. The symptoms begin as low as 8,000 feet and at 10,000 feet more than 75% hikers will experience at least some form of mild AMS. At sea level the percentage of oxygen is about 21%. At 12,000 feet, there are roughly 40% fewer oxygen molecules per breath. You are virtually inhaling twice to get the same amount of oxygen you normally would get at sea level. Plus the higher you continue to hike, the less oxygen and more breaths needed to supply your body. Your body must to adapt to the lesser-oxygen environment.

Symptoms of AMS are:

Headache,

Nausea and dizziness,

Loss of appetite,

Fatigue,

Shortness of breath,

Disturbed sleep, and

General feeling of malaise[lxvii].

More acute symptoms include:

Bluish discoloration in the skin,

Chest tightness, and

Confusion.

Many people work hard in preparing physically for the Mt. Whitney hike only to find they reach a point that the body just won't respond when called upon for exertion at the really high altitudes. There doesn't appear to be a particular age, body type, fitness level, or attitude that is more susceptible than another. Some hiking groups even do several weeks of hiking at high altitude to prepare the body for the high altitude only to have some of the group still fall out from summiting due to the illness. I witnessed that on my first hike.

If you are very concerned about altitude sickness, you can visit your doctor and let him or her know of the intended hike and the altitude. Your doctor can prescribe Acetazolamide (Diamox) to help improve your breathing at the higher altitude and reduce the milder symptoms. He or she will probably direct you to drink plenty of fluids and avoid taking alcohol when taking the drug.

People do die from altitude sickness, so it shouldn't be taken lightly. There are two more serious forms of altitude sickness.

HAPE

HAPE is breathlessness caused by excess fluid building up in the lungs. One should not experience breathlessness while at rest. Fever can also accompany HAPE, as well as coughing a frothy spit. If you or someone in your group experiences any of these symptoms, it's time to get them started down immediately.

HACE

Fluid buildup in the brain is called HACE. This buildup causes confusion, clumsiness and stumbling. The very beginning of HACE may include quite unusual behavior up to and including laziness, excessive emotion and/or violence. Drowsiness and loss of consciousness may signal death is not far behind. If you or anyone in your party begins to indicate symptoms of HACE, it is almost past time to react. Get that person to a lower altitude IMMEDIATELY!

I mainly mention HAPE and HACE to let you know that altitude sickness can be extremely dangerous. However, in reading many posts and experiences of hiking Mt. Whitney, I have yet to find a case of HAPE or HACE causing death. BUT, the altitude affects each individual differently. You should understand that altitude sickness could be extremely dangerous and recognize symptoms in order to know the seriousness and need for action.

Acclimation Hike

Mt. Whitney is in the midst of high mountains. You can check out some high locations to help you acclimate prior to your main Mt. Whitney hike. Just north of Lone Pine is an ancient Bristlecone Pine forest. One can drive up to 11,800 feet just to hike around and acclimate. White Mountain peak is 14,240 feet for another location. I personally like to simply hike to Lone Pine Lake on the day prior to my main Mt. Whitney hike. It is only about 10,000 feet but it is just off the main Whitney Trail and provides a photo-op time for the lower trail. I always hike the lower portion of the trail on my main hike in the early morning when it is dark. Hiking to Lone Pine Lake for my acclimation hike gives me the opportunity to take day photographs of the initial trail that will hiked in the dark in the following hours. It is beautiful and also provides an opportunity to practice using an ice axe and crampons as well as just having a great picnic.

Minimizing AMS symptoms

Acute mountain sickness or altitude sickness is the one enemy that may keep you from reaching your goal, the summit. If you want to give yourself the best opportunity to accomplish your goal, consider the following for your hike:

1. Make an acclimation hike to begin getting your body used to less oxygen.
2. Feed your body well and constantly. Begin with a good breakfast before you hike and eat at every rest. Even if you aren't really hungry, remind yourself of how many calories you have burned and need to replace.
3. Constantly and I mean, constantly, drink water on your hike. If you haven't consumed about 3 liters when you reach Trail Camp, beware! You may be dehydrated and don't even know it. Start drinking water early and frequently.
4. Take aspirin or ibuprofen before you start your hike at the Portal and again about Trail Camp or Trail Crest. Hopefully, this will help dull any headache you may get and keep you focused.
5. Take your time getting to Trail Camp. The first six miles of your hike is the easiest to race up the mountain. If you take your time on the initial portion of the ascent, you will give your body time to adjust to the altitude. If you want to race, do it from Trail Crest to the summit. At least your body would have time to adjust and by this time, I think

you may have different idea about how fast you want to make it to the top.

6. If you reach that point that you just can't go any further, recognize it and start back down. If you want to just rest where you are until your group gets to the summit and meets you at that spot, fine. If you decide you want to go down a ways to feel better, let your group know your plans or have someone accompany you down to your rendezvous point.

Of all the issues and concerns regarding hiking Mt. Whitney, acute mountain sickness is a major concern that may out-shadow all the other issues. It has no particular age, body size, physical preparation or any other specific to identify who will be able to make it to the summit and who won't.

GIARDIA LAMBLIA

"Giardia lamblia is a genus of anaerobic flagellated protozoan parasites of the phylum Diplomonada that colonize and reproduce in the small intestines, causing giardiasis"[lxviii] You may have also heard this called "Montezuma's Revenge". These parasites get to one's intestines through ingesting or coming into contact with contaminated soil, food or water. Infected animals taint the food, soil or water via feces.

Symptoms

It may take as much as two days to begin showing symptoms after being infected. The symptoms include violent diarrhea, excess gas, abdominal cramping, upset stomach, and nausea. Dehydration and nutritional loss can create a strong need of concern. One can lose weight rapidly as well as the ability to fight infections. After 1-2 days of diarrhea, constipation for 4-7 days is very common along with the acute gas production. This can last from 2 – 6 weeks. It is totally preventable and something you won't want to experience.

Prevention

Person-to-person transmission of the infection occurs through poor hygiene and sanitation. Water borne transmission occurs through ingesting contaminated water. Typically, this happens from drinking water from inadequately treated surface water sources. The water on Mt. Whitney is totally untreated. **All water** should be treated or filtered for your consumption.[lxix]

CRAMPING

After reaching the summit and heading back down the mountain, one might think that it was a great trek and no problems. But you have spent a lot of energy and are quite fatigued. You might begin to experience some cramping as you get closer to the finish. Cramping is an unpleasant, uncontrollable contraction of a muscle. It is caused by fatigue, low sodium and low potassium.[lxx]

The typical portion of the hike one may experience cramping is in the downhill hike. After hours of hiking, your body will be fatigued. Many people mainly train to climb uphill. This means most of the muscle conditioning is to climb. After reaching the summit, the hike is mostly downhill. There are a few areas where you will hike uphill on your return but again; most of the hike is downhill. The downhill hike will almost seem effortless for a while since it is quite a relief from climbing. However, as it took many hours to ascend Mt. Whitney, it will take just slightly less to descend the mountain. You will have a backpack weighing between 18 – 22 pounds (some of your water will be consumed and a good portion of your food, reducing the weight of the pack), along with your normal clothing and gear. Your muscles will be somewhat fresh at the start of the descent; however, once you get below Consultation Lake toward Mirror Lake, you will be doing a steeper descent. Your muscles will get a really good workout. If you have fed your body well on the way up and continued on the descent, along with drinking plenty of water, and taking periodic rests, you may not experience any cramping.

Cramping can also be caused by exposure to large changes in temperature, dehydration or low blood salt. Other research indicates that some cramping can be caused by low blood sugar; which is associated with excess insulin.

Avoid low glucose concentration by eating food frequently. It will help prevent cramping.[lxxi]

When planning your food such as breakfast and all the little snacks up and down the mountain, you may wish to make sure your diet has included plenty of sodium either from salt or from the foods such as nuts. Cramping is not such a major deal except when you are almost through with your hike, it can be frustrating to start feeling your leg(s) begin to cramp for the last few miles. In the worst case scenario, just stop a few minutes, rest and then continue on. Elevating your legs will make them feel better and relaxing for just five minutes will make a big difference.

BEARS

Bear warning sign

When you travel the road up to the Mt. Whitney Portal, you will pass several signs indicating, "Active Bear Area". I have yet to see a black bear on Mt. Whitney, but a friend of mine has. The Forest Rangers will have you or whoever is the leader sign an understanding that you are required to keep ALL FOODS out of your car and if carrying food, keep it in your backpack. Overnight backpackers are required to have a bear-proof canister. The Forest Rangers will make a big point; as well they should, about removing coolers or other items from your car that bears might identify as having food. Anyone ignoring the rules may be fined or even invited out of the area. All campers must store their food in the bear boxes provided at Whitney Portal.

Bears are strong animals and can rip through canvas tops on cars or find inventive ways to enter a car if they perceive food to be in the car. Don't ever leave food in your trunk or back of the truck, even if it is covered. A bear has a phenomenal sense of smell and could probably tell you what food you had in your trunk last, even if it was several days ago (if a bear could talk).

Black Bears

Black bears are not as large as grizzly or brown bears but they can be a formidable size. They tend to weigh between 125 to 500 pounds. Black bears have good vision up close (their distance vision has not been tested). Their hearing is twice that of human sensitivity. Their smelling capability is extremely good. Black bears are considered one of the most intelligent animals, thus the concern about food in cars. Black bears can climb trees and are speedy compared to humans. They are capable of running over 30 miles per hour.

Hiking with Bears

There are two concerns when hiking in bear country. You never want to surprise a bear and you NEVER want to come between a sow bear and her cub(s). As mentioned earlier, bears have excellent hearing. When walking the trail, it is an excellent idea to make noise while hiking. If you are starting out in the dark, it is NOT a good time to put your iPod earphones on to listen to music. You should be listening for any noise and making good noises yourself. Whistling, clearing your throat often and any other noise you might be able to make to signal that you are on the trail can be helpful. For the first five miles, you will be in probable bear country. This would be wooded and brushy areas below the tree line. Once you enter the granite areas where the trees are scarce, you are less likely to encounter a bear since their food supply is typically in the wooded areas. As you hike in the early morning, keep looking to your side, up and down the mountain from the trail. The light from your headlamp as well as the sound you make will help signal bears that humans are present. They are not really interested in you but let them know you are there and don't surprise them.[lxxii]

If you are hiking alone and really concerned about meeting a bear, you can carry bear spray. It is very similar to pepper spray and works up to a distance of about 30 feet. As I stated earlier, I have yet to see a bear on Mt. Whitney Trail. I have not even seen evidence of a bear, but I trust the Rangers when they tell me that bears are there. Hiking alone can be a different situation than traveling with a group. In a group, some discussions seem to continually go on. A group makes noise just by being in a group. A lone hiker is much quieter. Therefore, if you decide to hike solo, make noise, clear your throat and let any animals in hearing distance know that you are on the trail. Should you encounter a bear, the bear spray could be an excellent deterrent should a bear be surprised and decide to attack. The bear spray may at least make you feel more comfortable on your hike.

Are Black Bears Dangerous?

I researched bear attacks to see, one, if any had happened on Mt. Whitney; two, if any had happened in California; and three, where the closest attacks had occurred and if there was any commonality with bear attacks in general.

There have been NO bear attacks on Mt. Whitney. In fact, I could not find ANY in California. The closest attack I could find was Lakeside, Arizona in 2011, on a 61-

year old female; Uinta National Forest, Utah, in 2007 on an 11-year old male; in 2001, on a 93-year old female, in 2001, in Mora, New Mexico; and in 1993, Fremont County, Colorado on a 24-year old male. The remainders of black bear attacks were in Canada and the East Coast of the U.S.[lxxiii]

Should you happen to encounter a bear, the first thing to do is evaluate the situation. Did you surprise the bear or did it come up on you? Are there cubs in sight? Once you have evaluated the situation, do not run. Running sparks a chase mode for many wild animals. The bear will be much faster than you are, especially at high altitudes. Secondly, stand your ground against the bear. Thirdly, if you have come between a cub and the sow, calmly move away so you can to give the bear a pathway to the cub. Lastly, if you have cornered the bear, try to give the bear an "out" from the situation. Move just enough to allow the bear to escape the situation. Except for creating a situation where the mother bear fears for her cub's safety, the bear is probably looking for food. It doesn't mean you have to give the bear your backpack with the food in it. Hopefully, you have packaged your food in sealed bags and it isn't attracting the bear. Stand your ground and the bear should decide to leave.

I have hiked Mt. Whitney four times, once totally solo and three other times either with a group or a friend. I carried bear spray each time and did not take it out of its holster. I will continue to hike Mt. Whitney with friends or solo. My main concern in a bear encounter is for the first three hours, to just about Consultation Lake or just above Trailside Meadows. The areas below this point have good vegetation that would be more conducive to bears.

If you look at the California flag, you will notice that a Grizzly Bear is pictured. The last grizzly bear in California was shot in 1922.[lxxiv] They have not been reintroduced to the state. I do not consider a grizzly bear to be a threat anywhere in the state.

Side Note Regarding Mountain Lions

I have not heard of any sightings of mountain lions on Mt. Whitney. You should be aware that they are becoming more prevalent in California and it is just a matter of time until one is encountered on Mt. Whitney.

Mountain lions would most likely stay in the high altitudes to avoid too much confrontation with the bear population. They have food "on top" in marmots, mice and squirrels. However, I'm not sure that the food supply would maintain a mountain lion population. Any encountered cats may be just passing through the area.

Should you encounter a mountain lion, just as with bears, DO NOT RUN! They are large cats and just like you know of house cats, they will chase anything that runs. You would want to stand your ground and look as big and large as possible. Just remember that ANY animal doesn't really want to fight. If they hunting for food, they would prefer something to just swat and then they get to eat it. If they have to fight another animal, they just aren't really excited about it. They will make a big fuss, but you are probably taller than they are even if they could stand up. Yell and scream at the cat and it will probably leave. JUST DON"T RUN away from it! If you do spot one, report it to the Forest Rangers.

HIGHEST MOUNTAINS IN THE UNITED STATES

The following is a list of the tallest mountains by state. They are listed in descending order.

State	Mountain	Elevation (feet)
Alaska	Mt. McKinley	20,320
California	Mt. Whitney	14,505
Colorado	Mt. Elbert	14,440
Washington	Mt. Rainier	14,417
Wyoming	Gannett Peak	13,809
Hawaii	Mauna Kea	13,803
Utah	Kings Peak	13,518
New Mexico	Wheeler Peak	13,167
Nevada	Boundary Peak	13,147
Montana	Granite Peak	12,807
Arizona	Humphreys Peak	12,637
Idaho	Borah Peak	12,668
Oregon	Mt. Hood	11,249
Texas	Guadalupe Peak	8,751
South Dakota	Harney Peak	7,244
North Carolina	Mt. Mitchell	6,684
Tennessee	Clingmans Dome	6,643
New Hampshire	Mt. Washington	6,288
Virginia	Mt. Rogers	5,729
Nebraska	Panorama Point	5,427
New York	Mt. Marcy	5,343
Maine	Mt. Katahdin	5,270
West Virginia	Spruce Knob	4,862
Georgia	Brasstown Bald	4,784
Oklahoma	Black Mesa	4,975
Vermont	Mt. Mansfield	4,395
Kentucky	Black Mountain	4,145
Kansas	Mt. Sunflower	4,041
South Carolina	Sassafras Mountain	3,560
Massachusetts	Mt. Greylock	3,489
North Dakota	White Butte	3,508
Maryland	Hoye-Crest	3,360
Pennsylvania	Mt. Davis	3,213
Arkansas	Magazine Mountain	2,753
Alabama	Cheaha Mountain	2,413

Connecticut	Mt. Frissell	2,379
Minneapolis	Eagle Mountain	2,302
Michigan	Mt. Arvon	1,979
Wisconsin	Timms Hill	1,951
New Jersey	High Point	1,802
Missouri	Taum Sauk Mountain	1,772
Iowa	Hawkeye Point	1,671
Ohio	Campbell Hill	1,549
Indiana	Hoosier Hill	1,257
Illinois	Charles Mound	1,235
Rhode Island	Jerimoth Hill	811
Mississippi	Woodall Mountain	807
Louisiana	Driskill Mountain	535
Florida	Britton Hill	345
Delaware	Ebright Azimuth	447[lxxv]

Wikipedia, the free encyclopedia, List of U.S. States by Elevation,
http://en.wikipedia.org/wiki/list of U.S. states by elevation,
May 29, 2012, 1:20:00.

SIERRA MOUNTAIN RANGE APPEARANCE

If you are driving up or down US 395 and looking for a gigantic mountain that is very majestic, standing well above all the other mountains, you absolutely won't find Mt. Whitney! It doesn't stand alone like Mt. Shasta or Mt. Rainier. It won't be snow-capped to provide a picturesque vista. It will be camouflaged among a bunch of peaks that run for miles along a similar ridge. The whole mountain range is beautiful and is very similar to many other mountains along the Sierra range, looking like a saw-tooth. The Spanish word, "sierra" means, "saw".[lxxvi]

The land which would later form the Sierras was initially covered by ocean between 400 million to about 130 million years ago. The plates or surface of the earth was much like a jigsaw puzzle with pieces moving on top of the earth's inner core of molten magma. The Pacific Plate pushing against the North American Plate slid underneath it around 250 million years ago. The pressure and friction ground the plates and created tremendous pressure. The plates began to melt and formed plumes of liquid plutonic rock. This rock floated to the top causing a thick and massive line of scar on the earth's surface. The eastern side of the Pacific Plate began to rise gradually about 80 million years ago, while the western side from the North American Plate stayed somewhat constant. This caused uplift to be greater on the eastern side and the mountain range tilted toward the west[lxxvii]. If you would think of a board under a pile of rocks being stepped on from the western side, the slope would be gentle along the board. However, where the board left the ground and some of the rocks fell to fill in the gap from the board's up-swinging, you would see a gentle slope on the western side or board side and a jagged ridge at the top of the board. From the eastern side, the board face would appear quite jagged while the western side would appear to be somewhat smooth.

Flat Backside of the Sierras near Mt. Whitney

The above picture demonstrates the actual backside of the ridge just south of Mt. Whitney. West is to right. Not all the mountains along the Sierra Nevada range look like this. There are some areas with flat tops and other areas with curious shapes like Yosemite Valley which was created by glaciers. But when you see the jagged edges around Mt. Whitney and up and down the Sierras, you will know how they were formed.

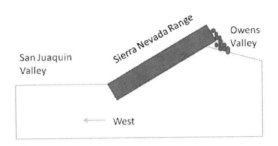

MOUNT WHITNEY

Mt. Whitney was named for Josiah Whitney, the State Geologist of California that participated in a survey of the mountain region. He was not the first to climb the mountain. During the expedition, another geologist Clarence King tried to climb the mountain from the west side but stopped short of his goal. King came back in 1871 to complete his task but from a different approach. He ended up climbing and summiting Mt. Langley. After King learned that he did not summit the right mountain, he again attempted and completed his goal in 1873. However, he was a month late to be the first recorded person to ascend the mountain.

On August 18, 1873, Charles Begole, A. H. Johnson, and John Lucas from Lone Pine, the closest town to the mountain, became the first people to reach the summit. They were fishermen and called the mountain Fisherman's Peak. With all the confusion, the U. S. Geological Survey Board on Geographic Names honored Josiah Whitney with the name Mt. Whitney.

Mt. Whitney Trail

The Mt. Whitney Trail was financed by the residents of Lone Pine. It was engineered by Gustave Marsh and completed on July 22, 1904. Unfortunately, just four days later the first recorded death occurred on Mt. Whitney. U.S. Bureau of Fisheries employee, Bryd Surby, while eating lunch, was struck and killed by a lightning strike on the summit. Due to this untimely event, Marsh began work on a stone hut that was completed in 1909 and is now known as the Smithsonian Institution Shelter.[xxviii]

Smithsonian Astrophysical Observatory (Smithsonian Hut)

The hut located at the summit was originally built in 1909. It is currently a refuge for hikers who look for shelter from the summit cold and wind. In the early 1900's, astronomers wanted to get above as much of the earth's atmosphere as possible. The highest mountain seemed a likely place to put a telescope and a building to shelter the astronomers. Donkeys carried the men and supplies up the mountain to build the structure. It took about four weeks to construct the 11 by 30 foot building. There is no wood in the building, just stone, cement and glass.

The main research for the astronomers was to study Mars. They were looking for traces of water on its surface. A sixteen-inch reflection telescope was positioned on the summit with a spectroscope. The scientists attempted to compare the spectrum of the Moon to that of Mars. They had previously determined that the Moon had no water and the comparison should provide information regarding water on Mars. The nights were bitter cold and the observing was disappointing just having two good nights out of several that was clear enough for observation. The continually stormy weather persuaded them to give up on the endeavor completely.[lxxix]

Lone Pine

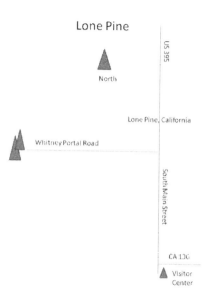

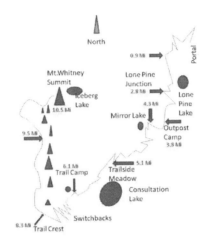

North

0.9 Mi → Portal

Mt.Whitney
Summit

Iceberg
Lake

Lone Pine
Junction
2.8 Mi → Lone
Pine
Lake

10.5 Mi

4.3 Mi
Mirror Lake

9.5 Mi →

Outpost
Camp
3.8 Mi

6.1 Mi
Trail Camp

5.1 Mi
Trailside
Meadow

Consultation
Lake

8.3 Mi Trail Crest

Switchbacks

MOUNT WHITNEY TRAIL MAP[LXXX]

198

YOUR TRIP

I've presented a plan on how to determine the best time for hiking Mt. Whiney, suggestions on getting your hiking permit, plan your trip, determine your necessary hiking equipment, have an idea of hiking concerns, ideas to enjoy this hiking opportunity, and understand more about Mt. Whitney. After reading the book, I hope you will look back on your preparation and feel that I provided good direction and helped you to be prepared for most elements of the hike so you can use the information to have a safe and enjoyable hiking experience. You should not have any major surprises and hopefully, you are able to plan a hiking agenda that produced tremendous fun for you and your group.

Ron Upson 19 ½ Hours Later

ABOUT THE AUTHOR

Marv Cope was born and raised in Sylva, North Carolina. He had no previous background of hiking before his Mt. Whitney venture in 2009. Marv trained for his four Mt. Whitney hikes at Livermore Valley Tennis Club. He is married and lives in Livermore, California.

One More Grin in 2012

ENDNOTES

[i] National Park Service, "Climbing Mt. Whitney", http://www.nps.gov/seki/planyourvisit/whitney.htm. April 26, 2012, 2:51:00.

[ii] Irvin Web Consulting, "Mt. Whitney Permits", http://www.mount-whitney.com/mt_whitney_permits.php , April 26, 2012, 2:50:00.

[iii] Paul Richins, Jr., *Mount Whitney,* (Seattle: The Mountaineer Books, second edition, 2008), 11.

[iv] USDA Forest Service, "Mt. Whitney", http://www.recreation.gov/permits/MtWhitney/r/wildernessAreaDeails.do?page=details&contractDode=NRSO&parkid=72201&topTabindex=Permits, April 26, 2012, 3:42:00.

[v] USDA Forest Service, http://www.recreation.gov/permits . April 26, 2012 4:03:00.

[vi] USDA Forest Service, http://www.recreation.gov/permits. April 27, 2012 1:38:00.

[vii] USDA Forest Service, http://www.recreation.gov/permits. April 27, 2012 2:17:00.

[viii] Huffington Post, http://www.huffingtonpost.com/2011/08/18/tyler-armstrong-7-years-o_n_930938.html. May 1, 2012 12:33:00.

[ix] USDA Forest Service, http://www.Fs.usda.gov/recarea/?recid=20698. May 1, 2012, 1:41:00.

[x] Richins, Jr., 140-142.

[xi] http://www.recreation.gov/permits. May 2, 2012 12:46:00.

[xii] Lone Pine Chamber of Commerce, http://www.lonepinechamber.org/lodging/lodgin.html. May 2, 2012 1:05:00.

[xiii] MapQuest, http://www.mapquest.com/print?a=app.core.d6ae61dfbbcb1e4c58bef25b May 2, 2012 1:48:00.

[xiv] Richins, Jr., 140.

[xv] Wild, Roger, British Mountaineering Council "Winter Essentials", "How to Ice-Axe Self Arrest", http://www.youtube.com/watch?v=lm3xlshmnnk. May 30, 2012, 4:19:00.

[xvi] Expert advice and tips on all aspects of walking /outdoors, http://timeoutdoors.com/expert-advice/walking-advice/winter-walking/how-to-use-crampons. May 24, 2012, 2:52:00.

xvii Elizabeth Wenk, *One Best Hike Mt. Whitney*, (Berkeley, California: Wilderness Press, 2008), 105.

xviii Wenk, 106.

xix Wenk, 107

xx Wenk, 110.

xxi Wenk, 111.

xxii Wenk, 113.

xxiii Wenk, 115.

xxiv Wenk, 117.

xxv Wenk, 120.

xxvi Richins, Jr., 140.

xxvii Topography Map, *Mt. Whitney, The Peak and Surrounding Backcountry* (Berkeley, California: Wilderness Press, 2008.

xxviii DayHiker.com, http://www.dayhiker.com/directory/MtWhitney.htm. May 7, 2012 2:30:00.

xxix Wenk, 99.

xxx Wenk, 100.

xxxi Wenk, 100.

xxxii Wenk, 100.

xxxiii Wenk, 100.

xxxiv Wenk, 100.

xxxv Wenk, 100.

xxxvi Wenk, 99.

xxxvii Wikipedia, the free encyclopedia, Mount Whitney, http://en.wikipedia.org/wiki/mount_whitney. June 2, 2012, 4:22:00.

xxxviii Wenk, 100.

xxxix Wikipedia, the free encyclopedia, Death Valley, http://en.wikipedia.org/wiki/deathvally, June 13, 2012, 3:50:00.

xl http://recreation.gov/permits

xli http://www.fs.usda.gov/recarea/inyo/recreation/hiking/recarea/?recid=20806&actid=50 . May 6, 2012 5:06:00.

xlii PubMed Health, http://www.ncbi.nlm.nlh.gov/pubmedhealth/PMH0001190/, March 22, 2012 3:17:00.

xliii Altitude Acclimation While Climbing Kilimanjaro, http://www.ultimatekilimanjaro.com/acclimation.htm. May 7, 2012, 2:23:00.

xliv Walker, John, http://www.fourmilab.ch/hackdiet/www/subsection1_4_0_7.html. May 10, 2012: 1:30:00.

xlv Wenk, 100.

xlvi Fitsugar, http://www.fitsugar.com/What-Does-SPF-Mean-Which-Sunscreen-Right-Your-Skin-3173539, April 13, 2012, 2:20:00.

xlvii Backpacker, http://www.backpacker.com/gearlistbackpackerhomemadefirstaidkit/gear/12113. March 1, 2012, 1:45:00.

xlviii Wenk, 70.

xlix Richins, Jr. 24.

l Richins, Jr. 244-45.

li Research Coordination Network, http://www.rcn.montana.edu/resources/tools/coordinates.aspx. May 18, 2012 6:23;00.

lii Travel by GPS, http://www.travelbygps.com/premuim/whitney/whitney.php, May 18, 2012, 7:02:00.

liii ESyderMedia, http://www.esydor.com/hiking_whitney_gear_list.htm. May 23, 2012, 2:37.00.

liv Travelby GPS. May 23, 2012, 3:18.00.

lv Richins, Jr., 142.

lvi Travelby GPS, May 23, 2012, 3:28.00.

lvii 5minLifeVideopedia, http://www.5min.com/video/how-to-self-arrest-with-an-ice-axe-166577575. May 24, 2012, 2:49:00.

lviii Fyffe, Allen, http://www.timeoutdoors.com/expert-advice/walking-advice/winter-walking/how-to-use-crampons. May 24, 2012, 2:52:00.

lix TimberlineTrails.net, http://www.timberlinetrails.net/whitneyweather.html. May 24, 2012, 3:31:00.

lx Top 7 Hiking Food Ideas, Stay Energized: Top 7 Hiking Food Ideas, http://www.hiking-trails-and-gear.com/hiking-food.html. February 29, 2012, 1:48:00.

lxi Consumer Research, http://www.consumersearch.com/headlamps/important-features. May 27, 2012, 3:51:00.

lxii All Things Photography, http://www.all-things photography.com/iso.html. May 27, 2012, 12:42:00.

lxiii Canales, Ben, "Get A Sample Shot", http://www.treehugger.com/natural-sciences/10-extraordinary-photographs-of-the-starry-night-sky.html. May 27, 2012, 1:00:00.

lxiv Random House Webster's Unabridged Dictionary, second edition, Random House, New York, 2001. 413.

lxv Wikipedia, http://en.wikipedia.org/wiki/hypothermia, March 28, 2012, 3:28:00.

lxvi http://en.wikipedia.org/wiki/hypothermia, March 28, 2012, 3:28:00.

lxvii Altitude Acclimatization, http://www.ultimatekilimanjaro.com/acclimatization.htm. May 7, 2012, 2:23:00.

lxviii Giardia, Wikipedia, the free encyclopedia, http://en.wikipedia.org/wiki/giardia, November 16, 2012, 1:31:00.

lxix Giardia, Wikipedia, the free encyclopedia.

lxx Cramp, Wikipedia, the free encyclopedia, http://.en.wikipedia.org/wiki/cramp. March 31, 2012, 1:43:00.

lxxi http://en.wikipedia.org/wiki/cramp. March 31, 2012, 1:43:00.

lxxii Quick Black Bear Facts, http://www.bear.org/website/index.php?option=comcontent&task=view&id=168&itemid=38. March 26, 2012, 1:59:00.

lxxiii List of Fatal Bear Attacks in North America, http://en.wikipedia.org/wiki/listoffatalbearattacksinnorthamerica#blackbear. March 26, 2012, 2:05:00.

lxxiv Grizzly Bear-Wikipedia, the free encyclopedia, http://en.wikipedia.org/wiki/grizzlybear. March 26, 2012, 1:54:00.

lxxv Wikipedia, the free encyclopedia, List of U.S. States by Elevation, http://en.wikipedia.org/wiki/list_of_U.S._states_by_elevation, May 29, 2012, 1:20:00.

lxxvi Wikipedia, the free encyclopedia, Sierra Mountains, http://en.wikipedia.org/wiki/sierra.mountains, June 1, 2012, 3:28:00.

lxxvii Resendes, Mary Ann, Central Sierra Nevada Society, Geology Of The Sierra Nevadas, http://sierrahistorical.org/geology-sierra-nevadas. June 1, 2012, 1:18:00.

lxxviii Mount Whitney, Wikipedia, the free encyclopedia, http://en.wikipedia.rog/wiki/mount_whitney. June 2, 2012, 4:22:00.

lxxix Smithsonian Magazine, "Around the Mall", http://blogs.smithsonianmag.com/aroundthemall/2009/08/the-mount-whitney-hut-turns-100/, June 17, 2012, 11:02:00.

lxxx Wenk, 102.

Made in the USA
San Bernardino, CA
08 June 2017